Critical Race Theory in England

Critical Race Theory (CRT) explains and challenges the persistence of racial discrimination throughout the world today, addressing issues such as racism, post-colonialism and systems of apartheid. Despite claims we live in a post-racial era, equality laws are under threat in the UK and evidence of racism persists in life and work.

This collection is the result of ongoing work in this area by a group of UK based academics: the CRT in the UK Discussion Group, convened by Namita Chakrabarty, John Preston and Lorna Roberts. The aim of this book is to examine the practical application of CRT within a specifically English context. Encompassing a range of fields, from education to civil defence, it considers the tools and techniques of CRT (including CRT feminist thought), from counter-narrative to the role of political positioning, but above all it analyses the workings of on-going racism within English institutions and structures.

Key aspects of post-9/11 culture are also critiqued and explored, including an analysis of Islamophobia and anti-racism, how counter-terror measures may reinforce racist beliefs, the role of race and the BME academic, and the manipulation of race in debates surrounding education and class. These new perspectives offer greater insight into the crucial area of race without which any understanding of 21st century England is incomplete.

This book was originally published as a special issue of *Race, Ethnicity and Education*.

Namita Chakrabarty is a Tutor in Creative Writing at Ruskin College, Oxford, UK. Namita worked on both the creative and business sides of the entertainment industry before moving into teaching drama and then lecturing in higher education. Her creative practice involves recorded and live performance besides creative and critical writing, exploring themes of race, sexuality and culture. Recent writing is included in *New Writing Dundee* (2012) and in *RIDE: the Journal of Applied Theatre and Performance* (2011). Namita is co-convenor of the Critical Race Theory in the UK Discussion Group.

Lorna Roberts is a Research Fellow in the Education and Social Research Institute at Manchester Metropolitan University, UK. Her research interests lie in the area of race, ethnicity and education, and she has been involved in several funded research projects. Lorna organised the first ever Critical Race Theory seminar in the UK, held at MMU, and was instrumental in establishing the UK based Critical Race Theory Discussion Group with colleagues Namita Chakrabarty and John Preston.

John Preston is Professor of Education in the Cass School of Education and Communities, University of East London, UK. He is the author of *Whiteness and Class in Education* (2007) and the co-editor of *Intersectionality and Race in Education* (2012, with Kalwant Bhopal). He has written and published widely on whiteness studies, education and disaster pedagogy.

Critical Race Theory in England

Edited by
**Namita Chakrabarty, Lorna Roberts and
John Preston**

LONDON AND NEW YORK

First published 2014
by Routledge
2 Park Square, Milton Park, Abingdon, Oxon, OX14 4RN

Simultaneously published in the USA and Canada
by Routledge
711 Third Avenue, New York, NY 10017

Routledge is an imprint of the Taylor & Francis Group, an informa business

British Library Cataloguing in Publication Data
A catalogue record for this book is available from the British Library

ISBN13: 978-0-415-71307-8

Typeset in Times New Roman
by Taylor & Francis Books

Publisher's Note
The publisher accepts responsibility for any inconsistencies that may have arisen during the conversion of this book from journal articles to book chapters, namely the possible inclusion of journal terminology.

Disclaimer
Every effort has been made to contact copyright holders for their permission to reprint material in this book. The publishers would be grateful to hear from any copyright holder who is not here acknowledged and will undertake to rectify any errors or omissions in future editions of this book.

Contents

Citation Information

The chapters in this book were originally published in *Race, Ethnicity and Education*, volume 15, issue 1 (January 2012). When citing this material, please use the original page numbering for each article, as follows:

Chapter 7

What's the point? Anti-racism and students' voices against Islamophobia
Shirin Housee
Race, Ethnicity and Education, volume 15, issue 1 (January 2012) pp. 101-120

Chapter 8

'You got a pass, so what more do you want?': race, class and gender intersections in the educational experiences of the Black middle class
David Gillborn, Nicola Rollock, Carol Vincent and Stephen J. Ball
Race, Ethnicity and Education, volume 15, issue 1 (January 2012) pp. 121-139

Please direct any queries you may have about the citations to
clsuk.permissions@cengage.com

Notes on Contributors

Stephen J. Ball, University of London, UK

Charlotte Chadderton, University of East London, UK

Namita Chakrabarty, Ruskin College, Oxford, UK

David Gillborn, University of Birmingham, UK

Shirin Housee, University of Wolverhampton, UK

Kevin Hylton, Leeds Metropolitan University, UK

John Preston, University of East London, UK

Lorna Roberts, Manchester Metropolitan University, UK

Nicola Rollock, University of Birmingham, UK

Carol Vincent, University of London, UK

Paul Warmington, University of Birmingham, UK

INTRODUCTION

Critical Race Theory in England

In England, Critical Race Theory (CRT) is emerging as a focus point for work on race in the educational context, although compared to its birthplace in the USA it is in its infancy. It has faced struggles which are particular to its national context. It has been negatively critiqued by Marxists (Cole 2009; Cole & Maisuria 2007), been confronted with 'white working class' identity projects (Collins 2004), and from critiques that suggest there is something particular and peculiar about racial oppression in the US (Kaufman 2005). If, as Ladson-Billings suggests, 'in its adolescence CRT takes on an international dimension' (2006, xii), then it is important that CRT develops, both in the English context in terms of establishing an academic identity, but also as a means of proving and developing the credentials of an international CRT. This special issue of *Race Ethnicity and Education* takes issue with the exceptionalist positioning and particularistic critique of CRT and explores ways in which the theory can, and is, being applied outside of the US. Contributors from the English context examine ways in which CRT can be used and adapted to explain and resist pervasive forms of racism. The special issue is edited by the conveners of the CRT discussion group in the UK, Lorna Roberts, Namita Chakrabarty and John Preston.

The articles in the special issue are wide ranging and cover history, activism, pedagogy, methodology and theory. In some senses there is little difference between CRT as practiced in England and the United States (perhaps because of the prevalence of structural racism in both countries) but in other ways the differences are evident whether that is to do with different histories or European theoretical inflections.

Perhaps key to understanding the differences between CRT in England and the US is the comparative histories of the two. Paul Warmington's article takes both congruence and difference between histories of race, racism and struggle between the US and the UK as its starting point. Whilst acknowledging the connecting points he points out the key differences in theoretical perspectives which mean that CRT inhabits a very different 'British intellectual space.' Kevin Hylton takes a different approach, focusing on CRT methodology rather than intellectual history, and considering the ontological positions of research in this area. Critically, Hylton considers that CRT is more than an 'application' of theory, or method, but rather a political positioning which involves the researcher in either transformational work or, ultimately, complicity. These aspects of methodology and researcher positioning are illustrated in Namita Chakrabarty's article that considers both absences and resistances for academics working with CRT using a complex mixture of texts. Key to this for Chakrabarty is the relationship between CRT and other theoretical frameworks, including psychoanalytic and literary theory. These perspectives show how some English work on CRT operates at a complex theoretical nexus with other theoretical perspectives and also reminds us that psychoanalytic perspectives (particularly through Fanon) and literary theory have inflected CRT.

Nicola Rollock's article uses a counter-narrative approach and uses theoretical conceptions of 'liminality' to critique conceptions of safety in white-supremacist academia. She develops *'Rules of Racial Engagement for (possible) Survival in WhiteWorld'* which demonstrate the daily reality for Black and Minority Ethnic academics in British academia. Far from illustrating the exceptionalist positioning of those who wish to denigrate the application of CRT outside of the US context, Rollock's article considers the reality that racism is endemic, global and micro as well as macro-political. Preston and Chadderton's article explores this further through the historical concept of the race traitor and whiteness, and Chadderton's work with young people on race; the article makes clear that CRT, as Hylton indicates, involves a conscious political positioning of the researcher, and as Chakrabarty explored, the theory of CRT is crucial to the analysis of inter-racial positioning at points of conflict or convergence.

Shirin Housee's work, from the personal perspective of a practitioner–activist as well as researcher shows how CRT analysis can inform the positioning and activism of British Muslims. It illustrates how CRT can re-inform personal histories and experiences outside of contexts they were originally intended for.

Finally, Gillborn, Rollock, Vincent and Ball demonstrate an intersectional approach to CRT through a large-scale study interrogating Black middle class parents' experience of racism as it impacts on their children in UK schools. The article critiques the current focus of UK educational policy on the white working class with its implicit 'intersecting raced, classed and gendered inequalities that shape the experiences of too many parents and children.'

References

Cole, M. 2009. *Critical race theory and education: A Marxist response.* London: Palgrave.
Cole, M., and A. Maisuria. 2007. 'Shut the f**k up', 'you have no rights here': Critical race theory and racialisation in post-7/7 Britain. *Journal for Critical Education Policy Studies* 5, no. 1. http://www.jceps.com/?pageID=article&articleID=85.
Collins, M. 2004. *The likes of us: A biography of the white working class.* London: Granta.

Kaufman, E. 2005. The dominant ethnic moment: Towards the abolition of 'whiteness'? *Ethnicities* 6: 231–53.

Namita Chakrabarty
Lorna Roberts
John Preston

'A tradition in ceaseless motion': Critical Race Theory and black British intellectual spaces

Paul Warmington

In the USA, where Critical Race Theory (CRT) first emerged, black public intellectuals are a longstanding, if embattled, feature of national life. However, while often marginalized in public debate, the UK has its own robust tradition of black intellectual creation. The field of education, both as a site of intellectual production and as the site of political struggle for black communities, is one of the significant fields in which black British intellectual positions have been defined and differentiated. This article argues that the transfer of CRT to the UK context should be understood within this broader context of black British intellectual production. Through a critical examination of race conscious scholarship and the diverse literature produced in the UK since the 1960s, this article identifies some of the dimensions of education that have been scrutinized by black British intellectuals. In doing so, it directs attention to questions being generated by the transfer of CRT to the UK and to the local materials on which those using CRT might draw, in order to build a historically grounded base for the development of CRT in the UK.

Introduction

One of the salient differences between the UK and the North American context in which Critical Race Theory (CRT) first emerged is that in the USA black public intellectuals are a longstanding, if embattled, feature of national life (Posnock 1997; West 2001; Banner-Haley 2010). However, while often marginalized in public debate and historical accounts, the UK has its own tradition of black intellectual production. The towering figures of the post-war era include CLR James, Claudia Jones, Ambalavaner Sivanandan, Stuart Hall and Paul Gilroy. In the field of education analyses of race and racism have been shaped by the work of Bernard Coard, Maureen Stone, Hazel Carby, Heidi Safia Mirza and Tony Sewell. Some of those named might baulk at the very notion of being described as 'black intellectuals' – but then it is probably the reflex action, if not the duty, of black intellectuals to strain against that descriptor and the myriad conflicts it invokes: tensions between speaking for 'particular' interests and 'universal' values; between independent thought and engagement in collective action; between representing 'the oppressed' and critiquing the injustices that exist even within their ranks. This article offers a contribution to two intersecting projects. The first concerns the potential for CRT and its conceptual tools to become embedded in the UK as resources to account for and to counter racialized processes in the field of education. The second project is to promote the need for educators, inside academia and beyond it, to acknowledge and draw routinely upon the black British intellectual currents of the past half-century. How might CRT articulate with theories of race, racialization and racism developed over time by black British thinkers? The black British intellectual spaces to which this article refers are not ephemera; they are rooted in historically specific dialogues with the disparate materials of pan-Africanism, Marxism, feminism, anti-racism, post-colonialism and post-structuralism. They have been inscribed in the pages of journals, in pamphleteers' ink and through struggles in specific schools, streets and town halls. This article identifies some of the dimensions of education that have been scrutinized by black British intellectuals and also considers education as a key field in which black British intellectual positions have been crafted. In doing so, it draws attention to questions being generated by the transfer of CRT to the UK and to the critical materials on which those in the UK using CRT might draw, in order to build a historically grounded base.

Notes on a 'tradition'

This article might be read as a variant of what CRT refers to as 'counter-storytelling.' Delgado and Stefancic (2001, 144) concisely define counter-storytelling as 'writing that aims to cast doubt on the validity of accepted premises or myths, especially ones held by the majority.' Solórzano and Yosso (2009, 134) emphasise that critical race methodologies, such as counter-storytelling, are designed to challenge 'ahistoricism and the undisciplinary focus of most analyses…analyzing race and racism by placing them in both historical and contemporary contexts.' They define the counter-story as:

> …a method of telling the stories of those people whose experiences are not often told …a tool for exposing, analyzing, and challenging the majoritarian stories of racial privilege. (Solórzano and Yosso 2009, 138)

The counter-story works through the assertion of agency, voice and history. The story told in this article is a counter-story in that it resonates with the voices of black British thinkers, so often silenced in majoritarian discourses of race and racism. Moreover, it insists on the historical agency of black intellectuals and the wider black and anti-racist movements through which they have often emerged. In asserting the 'historical dimensions of black life' (Gilroy 1993a, 37), it challenges majoritarian histories, in which black British people are depicted in passive, atrophied form as mere policy objects. This article offers a kind of meta-story, in that it suggests co-ordinates for re-telling the history of race and education in Britain since the 1960s: not primarily in terms of Acts of Parliament, policy reports, newspaper coverage or theories of 'race relations' but through the work of black British thinkers. I attempt nothing as crude as a homogenised 'black perspective'; these black spaces comprise analyses and arguments that are diverse, competing and shifting. As Gilroy (1993b, 122) remarks in relation to what the African American Marxist thinker Cedric Robinson (1983) termed the 'Black Radical Tradition,' if such a 'chaotic, living disorganised formation…can be called a tradition at all, it is a tradition in ceaseless motion – a changing same that strives continually towards a state of self-realisation.' Early in planning this article I dispensed with the notion of offering a tidy narrative history of post-war black British intellectual production. I began documentary research in key archives, such as London's George Padmore Institute, consulted growing online resources, including those of the CLR James Institute and the Connecting Histories Project, and returned to the major published works of the 1970s, 80s and 90s. As I immersed myself in these, I was simultaneously daunted and gladdened by the scale of the task: by the range and complexity of black voices speaking on education and by the hidden histories out of which spaces had emerged over time for conversation, critique, activism and dissent.

However, if I were to sketch notes on the history of black British intellectual production in the post-war era, what would populate them? Education, both as a site of intellectual production and as a site of political struggle for black communities, is certainly one of the significant fields in which black British intellectual positions have been defined and differentiated. It has rightly been argued that education was one of the key spaces in which the shift to a mass consciousness of being black British (or consciousness of the potential to become so) originated. That is, black Britishness became organic at the historical point at which black children, the offspring of settlers from the Caribbean, West Africa, India, Pakistan and Bangladesh, began to populate the schools (Stone 1981; Dhondy, Beese, and Hassan 1985; Grosvenor 1997; Phillips and Phillips 1999). There has long been awareness among black British thinkers that the haphazard development of education policies designed to address the needs and experiences of black children in British schools told a revealing story about the wider struggle to overturn perceptions of people of colour as an alien problem visited upon the (white) nation. For Sivanandan (1989) the *belatedness* of race equality policies in education and the tendency of those early initiatives to pathologize black children, families and communities defines race as a social relationship in Britain:

7

Policies is too big a word. There were no policies as such to begin with, except what grew out of the endemic racism in British society when labour was recruited from the so-called 'new commonwealth.' After the 1962 Immigration Act, when the doors were beginning to close and the workers sent for their families, schooling became a moot question. And yet the policies were directed at what various local authorities thought was overcrowding on the one hand, and ...'under-achievement'...on the other. Basically, 'Blacks' were seen as the problem, meaning both Afro-Caribbeans and Asians. ... There was no coherent, systematic body of thought or proper work being done about educating Black children. (Sivanandan 1989, 19–20).

In fact, as Sivanandan (1989) goes on to remark, organized work was emerging from black communities in Britain's major cities. So – to scroll forward – the field implied by focusing on black British intellectuals and education ranges from the early stands taken by the Black Educational Movement and Black Parents Movement in the late 1960s, which fed into the radical structural analyses of British schooling offered by Bernard Coard and Farrukh Dhondy in the 1970s. Coard (1971) and Dhondy et al. (1985) both drew in varying proportions upon their experiences of teaching in London schools, structural Marxist analyses of schooling in capitalism and the radicalism emerging across the black Atlantic, as well as their belief in the emergence of 'second generation' black Britons as an oppositional force. Carby (1982), much like Dhondy et al. (1985), saw black pupils and communities forming active opposition both to the authoritarian dimensions of schooling and the distractions offered by a facile form of multiculturalism, asserting that 'black youth recognize liberal dreamers and the police for what they are and act. ... Black youth have led the way in the redefinition of who's got the problem' (Carby 1982, 208). Such analyses should, in turn, be compared to the work of Maureen Stone and, later, Tony Sewell whose research was embedded in (to use Fisher's [2009] term) 'capitalist realism': that is, a rejection of radical 'deschooling' as utopian, combined with a rejection of liberal self-concept theories as being rooted in cultural deficit models. Both turned their emphasis towards school leadership as the key to improving the schooling of black pupils (though, unlike Dhondy, their focus was restricted to black Caribbean and African students). Stone (1981, 35) critiqued aspects of relationship-based teaching as a means by which the social structure continued 'operating through schools to reinforce the low status of black pupils.' Sewell's (1997) critical ethnographies were, in turn, critiqued by Heidi Safia Mirza (1999) as being constrained by an adherence to subcultural analyses and to the male lens. In the late 1980s and early 1990s the work of Mirza (1992) and Mairtin Mac an Ghaill (1988) on schooling and racialization began to draw upon notions of decentred blackness that derived, in part, from Stuart Hall's (1988, 1996) work on 'new ethnicities' and his rethinking of articulations between race, class and gender. These were cultural analyses in the truest sense, showing the influence of both Gramscian and post-structural analyses. In their concern with gendered modes of racialization Mac an Ghaill and Mirza countered the phallocentrism in which earlier accounts of resistance and opposition to the racialized processes of schooling were often embedded. Tariq Modood (1992, 2007), meanwhile, has persistently challenged dominant modes of political blackness and their reliance on both subcultural and Marxist analytical frameworks. More recently, research has emerged exploring the creative ways in which young people have negotiated 'in practice' the fragmentation, dissembling and reconfiguration of racialized identities in the UK. The research of Miri Song (2003), for instance, parallels similar work in the USA by Pollock (2004). Alongside these shifts has been intellectual work that has emerged from and fed into supplementary schools and community learning projects (Jones 1986), as well as thoughts on education growing out of older traditions of black labour activism (Prescod and Waters 1999) and pan-Africanism (Graham 2001). In addition to research explicitly on schooling, the very nature of academic disciplines, pedagogy and methodological inquiry – of what it is to be an academic and educator – has been radically reimagined by those who have, since the 1980s, drawn from the conceptual innovations of Hall (1988, 1989, 1996) and Paul Gilroy (1987, 1993a 1993b; 2000).

CRT: Atlantic crossings

CRT emerged in the USA during the 1980s as a framework for understanding the endemic presence of race within the American social and political formation. Its key analytical principles are aimed at countering the ideological claims to neutrality and meritocracy customarily proffered in fields such as law, social policy, news media and education. Through CRT analyses the 'taken for granted' racialized processes embedded in those fields are made visible. CRT is now well established in the USA through the work of academics and activists such as Derrick Bell, Gloria Ladson-Billings, Kimberlé Crenshaw, Richard Delgado and Jean Stefancic but it is a relatively new presence in the United Kingdom, where it has been utilized in the work of Gillborn (2005, 2006, 2008), Hylton (2009) and Preston (2010). In considering its US origins, Gillborn (2008, 26) has argued determinedly that:

> There is no reason. . .why (CRT's) underlying assumptions and insights cannot be transferred usefully to other (post-)industrial societies, such as the UK. . .CRT is very much a work in progress. . .. As with British anti-racism, there is no single, unchanging statement of what CRT believes or suggests.'

Nevertheless, this Atlantic crossing (which is yet another instance in the long history of intellectual exchanges within what Gilroy [1993b] terms black Atlantic culture) warrants critical reflection. One reason for scrutinising CRT's transfer is that North American CRT has uttered its key conceptual claims in both global and local registers. Thus, speaking 'globally,' Taylor (2009, 4) draws on Charles Mills' dictum that 'Racism is global White supremacy and is itself a political system, a particular power structure of formal and informal rule, privilege, socio-economic advantages.' However, CRT's 'local' origins lie specifically in the break with the American Critical Legal Studies movement made during the 1970s by legal scholars such as Bell and Crenshaw, who insisted upon the need for a *race conscious* analysis of race in US legislation, as opposed to slippage into regarding race as merely a technology of class (Crenshaw et al. 1995). Some of CRT's key analytical tools, such as interest convergence, contradiction closure and storytelling were crafted out of revisionist critiques of US civil rights law's liberal assumptions. In addition, the paper that more than any other signalled the transfer of CRT to the field of education, Ladson-Billings and Tate's (1995) 'Towards a Critical Race Theory of Education,' speaks CRT at this local level. So, for instance, its propositions around race and property include assertions that 'Race continues to be a significant factor in determining inequity in the United States' and 'US society is based on property rights' (Ladson-Billings and Tate 1995, 48). There is nothing peculiar about this; all social theory originates somewhere along the line in local observations. However, it does mean that we should pay due attention to the local materials out of which CRT might be crafted in the UK. Gillborn's (2005, 2008) critical analysis of whiteness and power in education has arguably signalled some of the shifts in focus entailed in the transfer of CRT to the UK. In particular, in Gillborn's analysis of education *policy* has tended to replace the focus on legislation that has historically driven the development of CRT in the USA.

CRT's robustness in the UK will be dependent upon taking the same kind of historically grounded approach through which CRT has been taken forward in the States. As such, rigorous CRT policy scholarship will make use of the historical materials of black British thought and activism. One of the salient contributions of Paul Gilroy to black British intellectual production has been his insistence on resisting accounts of race, racism and identity that 'suppress the historical dimensions of black life, offering a mode of existence locked permanently into a recurrent present where social existence is confined to the role of either being a problem or a victim' (Gilroy 1993a, 37). The assertion of black subjectivities in accounts of British history and society is, for Gilroy, vital to the project of transcending accounts wherein black people in Britain are rendered, within political discourse and practice, forever external and alien, drifting into public debate and policy at moments of crisis but remaining 'objects rather than subjects, beings that feel yet lack the ability to think, and remain incapable of considered behaviour in an active mode' (Gilroy 1987, 11). This emphasis on black subjectivities is, it should go without saying, utterly different to what Hall (1988, 28) referred to as 'the innocent notion of an essential black subject'; rather, it is born out of a concern that black people are understood as social actors, as history makers, as thinkers who are central to Britain's social formation.

The 'one millimetre' rule

The focus on black British intellectuals offers three highly contested terms for the price of one. Let me begin to unpack them by returning to storytelling mode. In early 2010 I attended the first John La Rose Memorial Lecture at the Institute of Education, University of London. Now as soon as I impart this information, I become aware of the need to consider how much contextual detail I should provide. For an international audience it is reasonable that I should explain something of La Rose's contribution to black British activism and intellectual life from the early 1960s up to his death in 2006. However, I do not have a clear sense either of whether, in the early twenty-first Century, I can assume common knowledge of histories of black activism with readers based in the UK, even taking for granted their interest in race, ethnicity and education. I might make reference to La Rose's work with the Black Education Movement: the London-based largely African-Caribbean initiative which, among its other activism gave rise, in 1971, to Bernard Coard's seminal *How the West Indian Child is Made Educationally Subnormal in the British School System*. This, in turn, might usefully direct attention towards the community campaigns against the banding and bussing of black (African-Caribbean and Asian) pupils in London in the 1960s. I might refer to La Rose's work in the Black Parents Movement and recall decades of parental campaigns against police harassment of young black people. I might cite his stewardship of the International Book Fair of Radical Black and Third World Books, which was a key driver of a now much reduced (at least, in the UK) network of activists, artists and educators. These are not mere asides; I include them to emphasise the constant necessity to make visible 'hidden' black British intellectual traditions (and, as in any intellectual space, there is always tension between tradition and radical, iconoclastic invention). There have been points when a momentum has been achieved in this respect: the mid-1980s, for instance, saw the republication of key works by CLR James, and the publication of Ron Ramdin's *The Making of the Black Working Class in Britain*, Buzz Johnson's biography of Claudia Jones and Peter Fryer's *Staying Power*. Additionally, I wish to signal that the history of black British intellectual production incorporates disparate strands, such as the work of bookshops and publishers (such as the Bogle L'Ouverture and New Beacon imprints), the Indian Workers Association, Southall Black Sisters, the *Race Today* Collective and the arts journal *Wasafiri*. It is not confined to the academy; indeed, it might be argued that black British intellectual life and academia have intersected only fitfully.

Anyway, whilst at the La Rose event a colleague whose experience of both academia and community activism dates back some decades recalled the expulsion of a body of black activists from a particular leftist group in the 1980s. He commented that the political party in question 'did want black members but if those black members were one millimetre away from their party line, they would rather not have them at all.' Needless to say, the 'one millimetre' rule does not apply only to 1980s Marxist groups. Indeed, it is not unreasonable to suggest that the extent to which black and anti-racist academics are taken seriously in 'mainstream' academia in the UK is often in inverse proportion to the extent to which their work draws upon radical black or race conscious thinkers. In academic research, for instance, the 'transgressive' Foucault has a legitimacy not necessarily accorded to Dubois or bell hooks. For commentators such as Young (2006), Gilroy's early, neo-Marxist contributions to *The Empire Strikes Back* are apparently more credible than his explorations of the intellectual histories of the black Atlantic. Similarly, some recent criticisms of the 'importation' of CRT into British education research have drawn a distinction between the 'pre' and 'post' CRT research of David Gillborn (Cole 2009). The brain drain of black British social scientists to the USA (Phillips 2004) may also be cited as further evidence of the marginal status of race conscious scholarship in British academia.

It is hard to calculate the educational losses that result from this conceptual and bodily attrition. The black British educator Maud Blair has written specifically about academia's residual suspicion of race conscious education research (cf. Warmington 2009) and tendencies for the work of black thinkers to be trivialised as special pleading, as lacking neutrality. She remarks, in terms not dissimilar to those adopted by CRT scholars, such as Parker (1998) and Gillborn (2008):

> When our contributions are thus judged and dismissed from within an ethnocentric framework, it presents us with a real dilemma. On the one hand, we consider our work important and wish to disseminate it widely, and on the other we are conscious that in order to do so we have to work within disciplinary conventions...(that) are themselves non-representative and exclusionary. (Blair 2004, 249)

For race conscious scholars a minimum irreducible framework should be to insist upon and take part in embedding credible, informed, *well-read* consideration of issues of race, racialization and racism. This means that if, as educators and researchers, we are willing routinely to use Gramsci, we must also be willing to draw on and interrogate Fanon; if we routinely use Bourdieu we should also use Toni Morrison. Where we draw upon CRT we naturally turn to Gloria Ladson-Billings, Richard Delgado, Laurence Parker and Patricia Williams. However, we must go beyond these touchstones and also invoke intellectual histories in which black thinkers have wrestled with the particularities of Britain's post-war context. Well-read consideration of race should draw upon the race conscious analyses undertaken across the disciplines by Ann Phoenix (psychology), David Dabydeen (literature) and

Kobena Mercer (cultural studies). We should heed the educational research of Gus John and Audrey Osler. We should invoke the work of race conscious intellectuals, activists and artists who have worked outside of academia: Jeff Crawford, Leila Hassan, Gita Sahgal, Chris Ofili, Caryl Phillips and Julian Joseph.

At this point it is necessary to clarify what I am and what I am not attempting to achieve by using the category of 'black British intellectuals' and insisting on the need for adherents of CRT to build upon their diverse work. Firstly, in this article I have deliberately gone against academic 'good practice' by listing a large array of names, some better known than others, and some without biographical explanation. This is an effort not merely to advocate at a rhetorical level but to 'do in practice' the work of invoking black British intellectuals as reference points; at the very least, I would like to intrigue readers and their search engines. Secondly, I do not wish to claim these thinkers for some essentialist, ahistorical notion of blackness (this should be apparent from the fact that some of those I name would not usually be considered 'black'). I do not attempt to characterise them as crypto-Critical Race Theorists; neither am I suggesting that there is a charmed, self-sufficient space of black intellectual endeavour: Ron Ramdin intersects with EP Thompson; Zadie Smith intersects with Nabokov and Barthes. As regards the use of the word 'black,' I am not interested in narrowly categorising the individuals named or in delineating 'our side' as opposed to 'their side.' Rather, I wish to signify something about particular intellectual concerns and approaches: a determination to *account for* the social construction of race as an organising principle of human relations, not to evade race, racialization and racism by treating them as unfortunate marginal, aberrant experiences. Black intellectual work of the first order is subject-orientated in that it refuses to bind black people as problems/victims or to refashion the politics of race as murky, transient policy issues. If pressed, I shall also define black British intellectual spaces as those in which a concern with race (as a fully social relationship) and with dismantling racism is an ongoing project, not a checklist item.

The notion of black spaces remains salient, as Reay and Mirza (2001) point out in their research on black supplementary schools, another intellectual space (markedly black and female) whose history lies outside of academia. Drawing upon bell hooks, they acknowledge both the risks and potential value of black 'sacred spaces.' in which conversations, alliances and intellectual work are freed from the pathologizing pressures of whiteness:

> In the past separate space meant downtime, time for recovery and renewal. It was time to dream resistance, time to theorise, plan, create strategies and go forward. The time to go forward is still upon us and we have long surrendered segregated spaces of radical opposition. (hooks, cited in Reay and Mirza 2001, 96)

The most fertile black spaces, I might suggest, have enabled exploration of both the material and the imaginative dimensions of the social formation, and have recognised the obligation to *go through* race in order to dismantle racism (or, perhaps, to dismantle race itself) (cf. Warmington 2009). I am aware that not all black British intellectuals will (want to) tick all of these boxes. I am also aware that some will argue that I might have dispensed with the term 'black,' perhaps simply using (after Leonardo 2009) the notion of 'race conscious' analysis. After all, white thinkers such as Peter Fryer or Chris Searle should be included in the spaces I have defined. However, while I am all in favour of acknowledging the unstable, porous nature of these 'black' spaces I am keen not to lose entirely a focus on the history of intellectual endeavour by people of colour in Britain. One of my early encounters with CRT was at the British Education Research Association Conference 2005, where David Gillborn presented a series of photographs of CRT thinkers. It was a purposeful act of deconstruction of representations of intellectuals dominant in the UK, wherein theory is automatically assumed to be a white domain and blacks are assumed to concern themselves with other, more junior forms of knowledge. In order to challenge the claims to neutrality of academia and the media, it is still necessary to invoke representations of African, Caribbean, Asian and Arabic thinkers and theorists. In the UK Black thinkers are not expected to 'want to rewrite the history of the world' (Hall 1989, 25). Perhaps, in a future setting, the term 'black' might be displaced but, for the moment, we should not lose focus on tracing the work of George Padmore or Sivanandan or Avtar Brah – and their conversations over time and across the Atlantic with Walter Rodney, Angela Davis and Homi Bhabha.

Black and British

Speaking of black British intellectual spaces also draws attention to the perennial slippage in racial terminology that exists between the UK and the USA and its implications for CRT's transfer to the UK. In the USA the term 'black' is customarily used to denote people of African American descent. By contrast, in the UK the term has a more complex history and continues, depending on context, to denote *either* people of African and African-Caribbean descent *or* to signify via the discourses of 'political blackness' the assembly of African, African-Caribbean, Asian and Arabic peoples constructed in the post-war period of immigration – the collective sometimes referred to in the USA as 'people of colour.' As Gillborn (2008) points out when discussing the transfer of CRT to the UK, this is a discursive issue, not merely one of aesthetics, and 'part of the reason for the ever-changing series of labels that are used in this field is the nature of the issues at stake' (Gillborn 2008, 2). Since the late 1980s Hall (1988, 1989), Modood (1992), Gilroy (2000) and Song (2003) have all interrogated the homogenising tendencies of British political blackness. They have raised questions about the dominance within political blackness of certain forms of African-Caribbean maleness; the marginalisation of women; the relegation of South Asian voices; the invisibility of queer sexualities; the complexities of articulation between religion and race; generational and class differences; the under-playing of the agentive potential of fluid negotiation of ethnic categories. Although Hall's (1988, 1989) proclaimed 'new ethnicities' have not entirely replaced political blackness, they have modified blackness' claims and necessitated critical self-reflection, hastening the emergence of unstable, decentred blackness. At the same time, it is still the case that many contemporary black British intellectual currents are derived from the moment (or idiom) of political blackness, even where they take issue with it.

The relevance of all this to the transfer of CRT is, once again, one of historical and conceptual lineage. In the USA the foundation texts of CRT (including Bell 1980, 1992; Crenshaw et al. 1995; Ladson-Billings and Tate 1995) prioritised the racialized experiences of African-Americans. That African-Americans have remained the dominant focus of the 'core' CRT movement is apparent from the fact that 'offshoots' such as LatCrit, Queer-Crit and Critical Race Feminism have developed in order to apply CRT's framework in other spaces. In the UK Gillborn's (2005, 2006, 2008) pioneering application of CRT has generally emphasised his studies of African-Caribbean pupils in English schools and he uses the term 'black' to refer solely to African and African-Caribbean people. By contrast, Housee's CRT research (2008, 2010) has referred to black lecturers in the umbrella sense and has also explored the experiences of South Asian Muslim students. At present, it is unclear whether CRT in the UK will continue to house both depictions of black identity (doing so signifies an adherence, albeit qualified, to 'traditional' UK notions of political blackness) or whether quasi-discrete strands of CRT will emerge to address, for instance, Islamophobia.

In this article the term 'black' is used in a contentious, even provocative, sense: with its umbrella, political meaning restored. In part, this is because this article is concerned with *histories* of black intellectual production in the UK (and much work between the 1960s and early 1990s adhered to the uniquely British use of the term 'black'). I do not suggest that umbrella usage of the word exhausts all possible meanings of 'blackness.' Importantly, 'black British' signifies something far more radical than geographical location. As Procter (2003) argues, the emergence of the term signified a shift from being *black in Britain* to being *black and British*. Quoting Jim Pines, Procter (2003, 5) suggests that 'it involves a radical deconstruction of the idea that "blacks are an external problem, an alien presence visited in Britain from the outside."' During the settlement phase of the 1960s and then in the 1980s and 1990s, as fully settled and 'second generation' black Britons began to write their own stories, black intellectuals began to appropriate Britain and Britishness as the legitimate objects of their work. This refocusing, this new self-representation constituted nothing less than a deconstruction of what it meant to be British. Note Hall's (1996, 472) advocacy for:

> the logic of coupling, rather than the logic of binary opposition. ... You can be black and British, not only because that is a necessary position to take...but also because those two terms...do not exhaust all of our identities. Only some of our identities are sometimes caught in that particular struggle.

Nevertheless, it is important to own up to the biases and inadequacies of the term 'black British' and not to suggest that the term is always appropriate. For instance, the term does not always overcome the old tendency to conflate 'England' with 'Britain.' Most of the 'British' names I have mentioned in this article have been based primarily in England, not Wales or Scotland. However, this does not of itself indicate that a focus, CRT derived or otherwise, on black British intellectuals should only be concerned with black English thinkers. Procter (2003) has done much to extend belated conversations across English, Welsh and Scottish settings, as has, for instance, the writing of the Scottish poet Jackie Kay. That said, because of patterns of post-war settlement, the majority of black intellectual production in Britain in the period from the mid-1960s onwards has emanated from England and a pre-devolution context. Moreover, 'black British' has remained a preferred term among many because, in theory at least, it implies the possibility of a Britain comprising multiple ethnicities and has allowed a creative fuzziness around the issues of the (still largely unpacked) limits of 'Englishness,' 'Welshness' and 'Scottishness.'

The historical patterns of post-war black intellectual production also account for the bias in this article towards Caribbean thinkers (or those of Caribbean descent) and the dynamics of what Gilroy (1993) has termed the black Atlantic. Yet the spaces to which this article gestures are not 'African-Caribbean' in any exclusive or fetishistic sense. In historical terms it would be absurd to map black British thought in the post-war period without reference to Sivanandan, Gargi Bhattacharyya or Kenan Malik ('Asian' intellectuals all but, in various combinations, Sri Lankan, Indian, British, Muslim, Hindu and atheist – all having used the self-descriptor 'black'). Suffice to say, a historical definition of black British intellectual production, with all its untidy historical specificity and contingency, is preferable to a doomed ontological chase. The diverse range of current CRT derived work (Hylton 2009; Housee 2010; Preston 2010) suggests that CRT in the UK remains open enough to work with decentred, unstable notions of blackness.

Black intellectuals and the problem of loyalty

Banner-Haley (2010, 1) remarks that the complexity of defining what constitutes an African-American intellectual has generated a 'burgeoning subfield...given to the study of African American intellectual history.' This is in stark contrast to the British context where sustained focus on black intellectual history is rare, notable work by Gundara and Duffield (1992), Schwarz (2003) and Carrington (2010) notwithstanding. Banner-Haley (2010) wisely resists attempts at exhaustive definition, instead favouring a historically grounded account that focuses on the 'constant' issues that African American intellectuals have explored since Dubois' time but also on the social shifts that have led African American intellectuals to address different issues and questions at different historical moments. If we focus specifically on British (or English) education we can both distinguish between and relate to one another 'constant' and 'specific' issues. For instance, it seems reasonable to accept that the issue – in the 1960s and 1970s – of African-Caribbean children being disproportionately placed in what were then termed Educationally Sub-Normal (ESN) schools (as addressed in Coard 1971), differs in its specifics from concerns about the under-representation of black students in higher education that were raised in the 1990s. Defining 'constant' concerns is more contentious. Sewell (2009) argues vehemently that the overt racism experienced by black children in British schools in the 1960s bears almost no relation to the racialized dynamics that pervade 'post-multicultural' British education. For Sewell, the continuation over 40 years of, for instance, disproportionate rates of exclusion among black boys is a symptom whose twenty-first Century causes are quite distinct from their 1960s and 70s causes. In contrast Mirza (2007) argues that decades of superficial discursive shifts (assimilationism, multiculturalism, diversity) only conceal 'patterns of persistent discrimination, both blatant and subtle...the illusive chameleon nature of racism in education...changes its mantle over time...the more things change, the more they stay the same' (Mirza 2007, 114). Utilizing CRT, Gillborn (2008) goes further, naming the pervasive, 'conspiratorial' nature of white supremacy as a constant and arguing that, despite the contemporary rhetoric of social justice and cultural diversity, the function of schooling is not to counter racial inequalities but to maintain them at a manageable level.

To return briefly to wider notions of the role of the black intellectual, Banner-Haley (2010, 2) argues that, historically, African American intellectuals have been, above all, *public* intellectuals. This is certainly true of CRT's proponents and of, in large majority, black British intellectuals as diverse as Sivanandan, the black Marxist, Maureen Stone, the liberal system adaptor, or Gilroy, the advocate of 'post-racial' conviviality. However, invoking the archetype of the politically engaged public intellectual, as CRT thinkers such as Delgado and Stefancic (2001) regularly do, does not exempt black intellectuals from the dilemmas explored by Dubois, Fanon or Said – or, for that matter Gramsci, Kristeva and Arendt. In discussing the 'problematic' location of black intellectuals, Posnock (1997) identifies a perennial dilemma between, on the one hand, the obligation to speak 'for' black people against a racist society and, on the other, the rejection of the fetishisation of black authenticity. Posnock (1997) perceives, in WEB Dubois' perpetual negotiation of the duty to bear witness for African

Americans (that is, to *speak of* race and racism) and his parallel concern to deconstruct the 'veil' of race (that is, to speak, *against race*), the emergence of the black intellectual as a 'social type...resisting the lure of the prevailing ideology of the authentic.' Dubois' often overlooked theorization of the black intellectual is post- and anti-racial in that it 'renders incoherent a need to be true to a prior essence – be it abstract humanism or unalloyed blackness' (Posnock 1997, 324).

The rejection of the burden of black authenticity intersects with what Edward Said describes as 'the challenge of the intellectual life...found in dissent against the status quo at a time when the struggle on behalf of under-represented and disadvantaged groups seems so unfairly weighted against them' (Said 1996, xvii). In *Representations of the Intellectual* Said (1996, 13) defines intellectuals, whether 'universal' or 'organic,' as individuals with 'a vocation for the art of representing...it is publicly recognizable and involves both commitment and risk.' For Said, among the greatest of these risks is the intellectual's relationship to nationalism, to community ('the intellectual is beset and remorselessly challenged by the problem of loyalty,' Said 1996, 40). However, for black British intellectuals focusing on education, problems of loyalty apply not only to their relationships to black communities but equally to the dilemmas experienced as educators who are part implicated in the sector's racialized processes and outcomes. In short, how critical should a critic of the education system be? Are we obliged to uproot the system or to evaluate and renew it? Over the past 50 years black British intellectuals have divided over these issues. For Carby (1982) and Dhondy et al. (1985), confidence in the instability of British capitalism inspired a rejection of a system they regarded as irredeemably complicit in capitalist domination and reproduction. In contrast, Coard (1971), even as he decried the structural racism of the education sector, offered guidance on how to improve schooling for back pupils. At opposite ends of the neo-liberal era Stone (1981) and Sewell (2009) have taken education in capitalism as a given, arguing for system adaptation (and in Sewell's case a kind of moral reformism). Elsewhere battle lines are more provisionally marked. John (2006), in language that partly harks back to the Black Education Movement and partly prefigures the small state/big society rhetoric of the current British government, calls for a revival of 'independent organization and the self-empowerment of our communities,' emphasizing the need for greater reciprocation between black and anti-racist professionals and black working-class communities. Graham (2001) and Reay and Mirza (2001) seek, in community education and the supplementary schools, ways of nourishing the desire for emancipatory education that exists in black communities.

Conclusion

Ladson-Billings and Tate (1995, 62) conclude their seminal statement on CRT and education in the USA by stating that 'Critical Race Theory in education, like its antecedent in legal scholarship, is a radical critique of both the status quo and the purported reforms.' Black British intellectuals have long records of critiquing both the education sector's reproduction of racial inequalities and the limitations of the forms of 'multiculturalism' and 'cultural diversity' often proffered as a panacea. This article has pointed to some of the currents of black British thought, developed over the last half century, upon which CRT in the UK might draw. Furthering the black Atlantic exchange, race conscious scholars in the UK should take courage from the determinedly *public* role inhabited by critical race theorists in the USA, who have continued, as did their many precursors, to mould, nurture and sustain the archetype of the black public intellectual. As this special issue shows, CRT has begun to emerge as an organising space for race conscious scholars in the UK. Moreover, the growing presence of CRT in education represents, by the very nature of the educational space, a public declaration of intent. However, in concluding his first book-length exploration of CRT's potential, Gillborn (2008, 203) draws upon an interview with Stuart Hall in order to reflect on the divided loyalties of race conscious scholars who would intervene in the education system ('We are all captured, to some degree, by the very machinery of racism...that we seek to criticize in our work'). Gillborn (2008, 202) also re-emphasizes the role of the public intellectual, asserting that CRT 'places genuine social action at the heart of its enterprise...do not imagine for a second that an analysis of racism alone is a sufficient contribution to the struggle for race equality.' I argue that, in order to use CRT to help us 'struggle where we are,' we must turn to those black intellectuals who have endeavoured to work out where we are: those thinkers who have helped orientate struggles inside and outside of schools. This will produce a historically grounded form of CRT in the UK, one in which black people in education are imagined not merely objects of policy scrutiny but as powerful actors and radical thinkers central to British social life. In doing so, we renew anti-racist praxis.

References

Banner-Haley, C. 2010. *From Dubois to Obama: African American intellectuals in the public forum*. Carbondale, IL: Southern Illinois University Press.

Bell, D. 1980. *Brown v. Board of Education* and the interest convergence dilemma. *Harvard Law Review* 93: 518–33.

Bell, D. 1992. *Faces at the bottom of well: The permanence of racism*. New York: Basic.

Blair, M. 2004. The myth of neutrality in education research. In *The Routledge Falmer reader in multicultural education*, ed. G. Ladson-Billings and D. Gillborn, 243–51. London: RoutledgeFalmer.

Carby, H. 1982. Schooling in Babylon. In *The Empire strikes back: Race and racism in 70s Britain*, ed. Centre for Contemporary Cultural Studies. London: Hutchinson.

Carrington, B. 2010. Improbable grounds: The emergence of the black British intellectual. *South Atlantic Quarterly* 109, no. 2: 369–89.

Coard, B. 1971. *How the West Indian child is made educationally subnormal*. London: New Beacon.

Cole, M. 2009. *Critical race theory and education: A Marxist response.* London: Palgrave Macmillan.

Crenshaw, K., N. Gotanda, G. Peller, and K. Thomas, eds. 1995. *Critical race theory: The key writings that formed the movement.* New York: New Press.

Delgado, R., and J. Stefancic. 2001. *Critical race theory: An introduction.* London: New York University Press.

Dhondy, F., B. Beese, and L. Hassan. 1985. *The black explosion in British schools.* London: Race Today.

Fisher, M. 2009. *Capitalist realism. Is there no alternative?* Winchester: Zero.

Gillborn, D. 2005. Education policy as an act of white supremacy: Whiteness critical race theory and education reform. *Journal of Education Policy* 20, no. 4: 485–505.

Gillborn, D. 2006. Rethinking white supremacy: Who counts in 'WhiteWorld'. *Ethnicities* 6, no. 3: 318–40.

Gillborn, D. 2008. *Racism and education: Coincidence or conspiracy?* Abingdon: Routledge.

Gilroy, P. 1987. *There ain't no black in the Union Jack.* London: Routledge.

Gilroy, P. 1993a. *Small acts: Thoughts on the politics of black cultures.* London: Serpent's Tail.

Gilroy, P. 1993b. *The black Atlantic: Modernity and double consciousness.* London: Verso.

Gilroy, P. 2000. *Against race: Imagining political culture beyond the color line.* Cambridge: Harvard University Press.

Graham, M. 2001. The 'miseducation' of Black children in the British education system – Towards an African-centred orientation to knowledge. In *Educating our black children: New directions and radical approaches,* ed. R. Majors, 61–78. London: RoutledgeFalmer.

Grosvenor, I. 1997. *Assimilating identities: Racism and educational policy in post 1945 Britain.* London: Lawrence and Wishart.

Gundara, J., and I. Duffield, eds. 1992. *Essays on the history of blacks in Britain.* Avebury: Aldershot.

Hall, S. 1988. New ethnicities. In *Black film/ British cinema: ICA document 7,* ed. K. Mercer. London: Institute of Contemporary Arts.

Hall, S. 1989. Ethnicity: Identity and difference. Speech to Hampshire College, Amherst, Massachusetts, Spring 1989. http://www.csus.edu/indiv/l/leekellerh/Hall,%20Ethnicity_Identity_and_Difference.pdf.

Hall, S. 1996. What is this 'black' in black popular culture? In *Stuart Hall: Critical dialogues in cultural studies,* ed. D. Morley and K. Chen, 465–75. Abingdon: Routledge.

Housee, S. 2008. Should ethnicity *matter* when teaching about 'race' and racism in the classroom? *Race Ethnicity and Education* 11, no. 4: 415–28.

Housee, S. 2010. When silences are broken: An out of class discussion with Asian female students. *Educational Review* 62, no. 4: 421–34.

Hylton, K. 2009. *'Race' and sport: Critical race theory.* Abingdon: Routledge.

John, G. 2006. *Taking a stand: Gus John speaks on education, race, social action and civil unrest 1980–2005.* Manchester: Gus John Partnership.

Jones, V. 1986. *We are our own educators! Josina Machel: From supplementary to black complementary school.* London: Karia.

Ladson-Billings, G., and W. Tate. 1995. Towards a critical race theory of education. *Teachers College Record* 97, no. 1: 47–68.

Leonardo, Z. 2009. *Race, whiteness and education.* Abingdon: Routledge.

Mac an Ghaill, M. 1988. *Young, gifted, and black: Student–teacher relations in the schooling of black youth.* Milton Keynes: Open University.

Mirza, H. 1992. *Young, female and black.* London: Routledge.

Mirza, H. 1999. Black masculinities and schooling: A black feminist response. *British Journal of Sociology of Education* 20, no. 1: 137–47.

Mirza, H. 2007. The more things change, the more they stay the same. In *Tell it like it is: How our schools fail black children,* ed. B. Richardson, 108–16. London: Bookmarks/Trentham.

Modood, T. 1992. *Not easy being British: Colour, culture and citizenship*. London: Runnymede/Trentham.

Modood, T. 2007. *Multiculturalism: A civic idea*. Cambridge: Polity.

Parker, L. 1998. "Race is … race ain't": An exploration of the utility of critical race theory in qualitative research in education. *International Journal of Qualitative Studies in Education* 11, no. 1: 43–55.

Phillips, S. 2004. Black intellectual seems an oxymoron in England. *Times Higher Education*, 29th October. http://www.timeshighereducation.co.uk/story.asp?storyCode=192064&sectioncode=26.

Phillips, M., and T. Phillips. 1999. *Windrush: The irresistable rise of multi-racial Britain*. London: Harper Collins.

Pollock, M. 2004. Race wrestling: Struggling strategically with race in educational practice and research. *American Journal of Education* 111: 25–67.

Posnock, R. 1997. How it feels to be a problem: Du Bois, Fanon, and the "impossible life" of the black intellectual. *Critical Inquiry* 23: 323–49.

Prescod, C., and H. Waters, eds. 1999. *A world to win: Essays in honour of A. Sivanandan*. London: Institute of Race Relations.

Preston, J. 2010. Concrete and abstract racial domination. *Power and Education* 2, no. 2: 115–25.

Procter, J. 2003. *Dwelling places: Postwar black British writing*. Manchester: Manchester University Press.

Reay, D., and H. Mirza. 2001. Black supplementary schools: Spaces of radical blackness. In *Educating our black children: New directions and radical approaches*, ed. R. Majors, 90–100. London: RoutledgeFalmer.

Robinson, C. 1983. *Black Marxism: The making of the black radical tradition*. London: Zed Books.

Said, E. 1996. *Representations of the intellectual*. New York: Vintage.

Schwarz, B. 2003. *West Indian intellectuals in Britain*. Manchester: Manchester University Press.

Sewell, T. 1997. *Black masculinities and schooling: How black boys survive modern schooling*. Stoke: Trentham.

Sewell, T. 2009. *Generating genius: Black boys in love, ritual and schooling*. Stoke: Trentham.

Sivanandan, A. 1989. Racism, education and the black child. In *Looking beyond the frame: Racism, representation and resistance*, ed. M. Reeves and J. Hammond, 19–24. Oxford: Third World First.

Solórzano, D., and T. Yosso. 2009. Counter-storytelling as an analytical framework for educational research. In *Foundations of critical race theory in education*, ed. E. Taylor, D. Gillborn, and G. Ladson-Billings, 131–47. Abingdon: Routledge.

Song, M. 2003. *Choosing ethnic identity*. Cambridge: Polity.

Stone, M. 1981. *The education of the black child: The myth of multiracial education*. London: Fontana.

Taylor, E. 2009. The foundations of critical race theory in education: An introduction. In *Foundations of critical race theory in education*, ed. E. Taylor, D. Gillborn, and G. Ladson-Billings, 1–13. Abingdon: Routledge.

Warmington, P. 2009. Taking race out of scare quotes: Race conscious social analysis in an ostensibly post-racial world. *Race Ethnicity and Education* 12, no. 3: 281–96.

West, C. 2001. *Race matters*. New York: Vintage.

Young, R. 2006. Putting materialism back into race theory: Towards a transformative theory of race. *The Red Critique* 11. http://www.redcritique.org/WinterSpring2006/puttingmaterialismbackintoracetheory.htm.

Talk the talk, walk the walk: defining Critical Race Theory in research

Kevin Hylton

Over the last decade there has been a noticeable growth in published works citing Critical Race Theory (CRT). This has led to a growth in interest in the UK of practical research projects utilising CRT as their framework. It is clear that research on 'race' is an emerging topic of study. What is less visible is a debate on how CRT is positioned in relation to methodic practice, substantive theory and epistemological underpinnings. The efficacy of categories of data gathering tools, both traditional and non-traditional is a discussion point here to explore the complexities underpinning decisions to advocate a CRT framework. Notwithstanding intersectional issues, a CRT methodology is recognisable by how philosophical, political and ethical questions are established and maintained in relation to racialised problematics. This paper examines these tensions in establishing CRT methodologies and explores some of the essential criteria for researchers to consider in utilising a CRT framework.

Introduction

This article focuses on what constitutes a Critical Race Theory (CRT) methodology. Over the last decade there has been a noticeable growth in published works citing CRT in the UK. This has led to an increase in practical research projects utilising CRT as their framework. It is clear that research on 'race' is an emerging topic of study recently encapsulated by the work of Seidman (2004), Bulmer and Solomos (2004), Gunaratnam (2003), Denzin and Giardina (2006a, 2006b, 2007), Tuhiwai Smith (2006), and Denzin, Lincoln, and Tuhiwai Smith (2008). What is less visible is a debate on how CRT is positioned in relation to the 'nexus of methodic practice, substantive theory and epistemological underpinnings that is a methodology (Harvey 1990, 1). These philosophical, ethical, and practical questions are initially considered here by examining the notions of ontology, epistemology and methodology before practical considerations of recognising, framing and applying CRT research methodologies are explored.

Tweed (2006, 20) suggests that theories, in the first sense of the word, are 'travels' and yet the journey to CRT[1] for many, has inevitably engaged and rejected many mainstream theoretical frameworks, pairing down, adapting and moulding ideas until settling with CRT (cf. Dockery 2000). CRT for many is a framework that explains issues and isolates realities in a way that many critical theories struggle with. Tyson (2003, 20) succinctly summarises how her experience and understanding of her everyday world led her to use CRT when she said:

> It is the understanding of lived oppression – the struggle to make a way out of no way – which propels us to problematise dominant ideologies in which knowledge is constructed.

CRT like other substantive critical theoretical frameworks is determined by an ontological position best outlined by its commonly held tenets and eloquently brought to life by Tyson. CRT's major premise is that society is fundamentally racially stratified and unequal, where power processes systematically disenfranchise racially oppressed people. Accordingly, we have a society where some are more likely to be looking up from 'the bottom' than others as a consequence of their background. Ontological positions ensure that activist-scholars remain conscious of the crucial social processes that structure their worlds and that they are prepared to consistently look 'to the bottom' for answers as well as questions.

CRT scholars are motivated with taking these ideas forward as the starting point for anti-racist, anti-subordination, social justice and social transformation activities. Importantly, such ideas apply to the research, epistemologies and methodologies that inform them. Where racism and the distribution of power and resources disproportionately marginalise racialised people's position in society, CRT ensures that they remain central to research investigations or critical lenses rather than at convenient margins. Where power and status is stacked against those groups that have been marginalised, Dockery (2000) is not afraid to say that he feels it is necessary to 'take sides' if they gain some advantage from his research. His aim to reduce practices that exacerbate inequality and racial hierarchies are in step with the ontological perspective taken by numerous CRT researchers such as Tyson above, Parker et al. (1999), Lopez and Parker (2003), Matsuda et al. (1993), Dixson and Rousseau (2006).

Currently many researchers are asking challenging questions by utilising off-shoots of CRT such as Critical Race Feminism (CRF), and Critical Whiteness Studies (CWS) in ways that centre particular problematics. These emergent fields of scholarship are developing critical centres of interest. Other off-shoots of CRT are well documented and reflect core issues for activist scholars informed by CRT and their own lived experience (Delgado and Stefancic 1999). CRT has influenced research that have become more popular in Britain, these include Whiteness critiques incorporating Cultural analysis (Chakrabarty 2011), Whiteness and Policy Analysis (Preston 2008; Gillborn 2005, 2008); Theoretical Critiques of CRT and Class (Warmington 2011; Cole 2011); and Theoretical Critiques of Policy (Pilkington 2011; Gillborn 2006); Pedagogy and classroom counter-narratives (Housee 2008); and the Black experience of Sport and Leisure (Burdsey 2011; Hylton 2003, 2005, 2009; Hylton et al. 2011). Many of these studies have engaged with education policy and practice and it is reasonable to argue that it was here rather than the legal profession where the original site of struggle for CRT in the UK began. It is likely that as 'crits' have developed in the US to respond to specific social issues then the UK is likely to develop its own account of UK and transnational issues as CRT is applied more widely.

In earlier studies, before CRT emerged in the UK, I drew my influences for methodologies from critical theoretical studies in fields related to critical black studies (Hylton 2003). However, in a comparative study of race equality in local government, like Dockery (2000) and Dunbar (2008), I came to the conclusion that traditional approaches to critical policy studies were incomplete and requiring a more critical 'race' focused perspective that spoke to my lived experience of equality in the public sector. In relation to this, Ladson-Billings and Donnor (2008) talk about the constant reminders they get of their 'otherness' which they term 'waiting for the call,'[2] and like Dunbar's ontological position, 'for as long as I can remember 'race' has been my center' (2008, 89). CRT offered a theoretical frame that enhanced my critical lens and enabled me to draw from other scholars unafraid to make bold statements about, and challenge, the racialised order of things.

In addition to local and central government, academia is affected by naturalised systems of order, especially where praxis is flawed due to episte-mological (in)consistencies that make claims to the nature and order of valid knowledge and science. CRT implies a critical epistemological root, though knowledge development has suffered from mainstream agendas that have neglected and negated new and emergent forms of research. For example Dunbar's (2008) observations of the precarious nature of researchers, and research, on 'race' reflects more their position in the academy than the qual-ity of their scholarship. Epistemologies are a result of social practices where power is being exercised that can reinforce colour-blind, 'race' neutral, ahistorical, and apolitical points of view. Leading Duncan (2006) to argue that this process is how oppression and inequality may appear 'natural.' Delgado Bernal (2002) concurs as she explores how the use of a critical race gendered epistemology can acknowledge black people as holders and legiti-mate sources of knowledge where Eurocentric epistemologies consistently fail. Knaus (2009) applies this principle in the classroom to facilitate the 'voicing' of black students, as Flores and Garcia (2009) use this approach to create safe spaces for Latina students in predominantly white institutions in higher education. Using the experiences of black people being centred and seen as valid knowledge in understanding their marginalization, alienation and power relations is now a common theme in CRT. Developing these ideas further, Goldberg's (1993, 150) view that 'power is exercised epistemologically in the dual practices of naming and evaluating', is best articulated in the research and knowledge that inform us. In practice, a CRT methodology can challenge narrow ideologies and this should be traceable through its implementation back to its theoretical roots.

A CRT methodology should in part be characterized by its ability to eschew the passive reproduction of established practices, knowledge and resources, that make up the way types of research have been traditionally carried out. The 'one size fits all' (Carter 2003, 31) myth is demystified at the same time as contributions to new and emergent forms of knowing become valuable outcomes of developing CRT methodologies. Collins (1990) and Dunbar (2008) exemplify this debate as they charge white social science with struggling to maintain the mantle of the vehicle in which to effectively explore issues pertaining to 'race' in society. Where Dunbar urges a challenge to white supremacy and privilege in wider society, Collins specifically urges us to do this by searching for ways to reflect the experiences of black people without borrowing passively from white social science. A CRT approach has the potential to facilitate a challenge to mainstream epistemologies and, consequently, their agendas.

> Methodology is thus at the point at which method, theory and epistemology coalesce in an overt way in the process of directly investigating specific instances within the social world. (Harvey 1990, 1)

To reiterate, the politics of inquiries should be traceable back through **methodologies** to the ideas that underpin them. It is argued here that CRT embraces critical research, though it is wary of their complacency and colour-blindness in that regard. Those researchers that advocate neutrality and objectivity, aligned to conventional views of validity and reliability may not agree that they could be reinforcing racialised inequalities by tolerating only certain forms of knowledge. In relation to neutrality and objectivity, CRT has been critical of mainstream methodologies for being apolitical, and reinforcing oppressions whilst subordinating the voices and values of those rendered invisible through conventional modes of thinking (Parker et al. 1999; Denzin and Giardina 2007; Denzin, Lincoln, and Tuhiwai Smith 2009). Tuhiwai Smith (2006b, 2) exemplifies this in her work on indigeneity in the Southern hemisphere as she emphasises the institutional silence and silencing of indigenous peoples/issues. 'Research is a site of struggle between the *interests and ways of knowing of the West* and the interests and ways of *resisting of the Other*' (emphasis added).

'Race', class, gender and their intersections have regularly been excluded from important social and political developments and landmarks in knowledge and dominant paradigms. As a result the use of 'voicing,' storytelling and counter-storytelling have become popular tools in the expression of a CRT standpoint. Critical race theorists recognise that stories or discourses have been the privilege of those historically influential in knowledge generation and research. Counter-stories however, can present views rarely evidenced in social research. Storytelling still has some weaknesses. Even with their cloaks of validity and reliability stories are socially constructed and can represent limited versions of reality for subjugated people and their everyday experiences, especially where oppressive social arrangements remain unchallenged. In these cases research on 'race' and racism can perpetuate the status quo and cloud the landscape with spurious 'experiences from the margins.' Professional environments too, with their shroud of authenticity, must not remain uncritiqued either because they regularly remain uncontested due to their ability to self perpetuate and validate such practices. CRT methodologies have the potential to contest traditional approaches to critical research especially where previous studies including the social sciences have challenged power relations *without necessarily* challenging racialised ones.

Critical race theorists are adamant that the body of work that informs a CRT epistemology is likely to be broad due to its emphasis on transdisciplinarity. Yet, at the same time, CRT necessitates a coherence of ideas and synchronous principles and propositions that underpin methodologies and resonate with critical race politics. The alternative hegemony of dominant ideas often leaves power relations uncontested and seemingly incontestable. A critical race consciousness must invigorate these arenas to disrupt the negative racialised relations of late modernity. It can do this by recognising that though CRT is a pragmatic framework and therefore without a pedantic set of methods or methodologies, there are clearly methodologies and approaches that can facilitate CRT politics. Even within this relatively loose set of propositions there are caveats. These revolve around knowledge formation and validation, the nature of 'scientific' rigour, and what constitutes suitable topics for disciplinary lenses.

Establishing a CRT methodology

CRT's pragmatic politics ensure that no one methodology is privileged, dogma is challenged even amongst activist scholars. However, what makes these agendas similar, as *identifiably CRT* in nature, involves a measure of commitment to social justice and social change, and recognition that 'race' and racism are central factors in the social order. A CRT methodology can be identified by its focus on 'race' and racism and its intersections and a commitment to challenge racialised power relation. For example, Blaisdell's (2009) shift toward using CRT came from an examination of teaching and the sociology of education. Here he came to the conclusion that the empirical research in the sociology of education that challenged liberal ideologies and a range of racisms was inadequate for him to pursue a more proactive transformative agenda. For Blaisdell, the solution was to utilise a CRT approach that challenged the liberalism of educationalists as academics and practitioners.

A question that activist scholars (and external examiners!) are likely to ask is 'how has a CRT agenda been centred in this methodology?' The politics of CRT research posit that there must be some impact on (or challenge to) negative racialised relations. Just as Glover (2009), felt able to ask different questions to those traditionally tabled about crime control to ones about racial oppression, it is incumbent upon each activist scholar, or intervention, to explicitly articulate this message. For instance, studies that test the notion of merit and racial equality in local government, racialised professional hierarchies in the accounting profession, racial disparities in stop-and-search techniques by police forces, the experience of underrepresented black teachers in UK teacher training, the experience of black children in early years, or even media representations of sporting bodies *can all* be pursuing some of the agendas of CRT. Therefore there is no one narrow methodological approach, nor a reductionist set of predetermined agendas. However, the *aim* of a study and the *tools* used to implement it will carry CRT researchers in the correct direction, *or otherwise*. By this it is argued that the *methods* and *implementation* of a study are just as significant as its *purpose*. CRT is described as a framework, however it would be more accurate to describe it as praxis, given that it requires a lived activism (Hermes 1999). What better than a research methodology to demonstrate how to walk the walk?

To reiterate, methodologies with a CRT identity are likely to be inclusive of essential criteria and possibly some desirable ones too. Like any theoretical framework, CRT is recognisable by properties that enable it to be recognised as so. The emphasis on the disruption of racism and negative racialised relations, the centering of 'race' in the problematising of social relations, underpinned by a social justice agenda and the transformation of negative social relations are fundamental to the identity of CRT methodologies. Dependent upon the issue under consideration there will be other elements from CRT that emerge in a more conspicuous fashion that would need to inform our understanding or negation of negative social arrangements. They may be for reasons of a more nuanced understanding of a complex issue in policing, education, the arts, or community work, reflecting the reality of society, presenting us with relatively simple to complex questions requiring responses of relative sophistication. How can a methodology demonstrate its particular focus whilst embracing the spirit of CRT? How can 'race' be centred and not ignored? How can racism or racialisation be challenged as outcomes of a study? Similarly, how can change to negative racialised relations be a likely result at the conclusion of any study?

There are other important questions that need to be asked in relation to what constitutes an identifiable CRT methodology. Researching 'race' is fraught with conceptual minefields that can empower and completely hamstring attempts to research and transform negative racialised relations. Of this issue, Gunaratnam (2003, 5) highlights key questions for CRT research, these are: How can we make decisions about the points at which we 'fix' the meanings of racial and ethnic categories in order to *do* empirical research? Though these issues are not only pertinent to those adopting a CRT approach to research, they are necessarily unavoidable concerns for those who centre 'race' in their scholarly activities. Judgements about the epistemological and political repercussions of utilising this concept have to be made. Similarly the impact of ignoring 'raced' realities is too large an issue to ignore too. For instance, in research concerning *privileging* the black voice, counter-storytelling and chronicling marginalised accounts, a CRT approach should recognise these lived experiences whilst operating an anti-essentialist frame to confront accusations of homogenisation, over-generalisation and reductionism. To ignore these criticisms is to undermine the work of critical race theorists in the most fundamental of ways, and would marginalise even further some of the crucial debates emerging in the social sciences concerning intersectionality and the influence of social and cultural arrangements upon them. As emerging debates, their marginalisation would sideline the developments around 'mixed race' identities (Song 2004, 2010); 'race,' class and their intersections (Cole 2009; Gillborn 2009); 'race,' gender and their intersections and related debates around intersection-alities (Crenshaw 1995; Crenshaw et al. 1995; Ludvig 2006; Phoenix and Pattynama 2006; Hankivsky et al. 2010). It is necessary to state that class and gender theories contribute to CRT as they inform the nuances of inter-sectionality. However, Solorzano and Yosso emphasise the centrality of 'race' and racism in CRT methodologies when they state that:

> Critical race theory advances a strategy to foreground and account for the role of race [sic] and racism. . .and works toward the elimination of racism as part of a larger goal of opposing or eliminating other forms of subordination based on gender, class, sexual orientation, language and national origin. (Solorzano & Yosso 2002, 25)

The anti-essentialism of the intersectionality thesis strengthens a CRT frame-work especially as the CRT emphasis on centering 'race' can be miscon-strued as essentialism. Intersectionality is one of the mechanisms used in CRT to emphasise that though the starting point for CRT is 'race' and rac-ism there is no intention to lose sight of the complexities of the intersection of 'race' with the constructed and identity related nature of other forms of oppression. Intersectionality is concerned with the tensions of research that consider single issue research, in addition to examining overlapping and lived axes of oppression (Hankivsky and Christoffersen 2008; Hankivsky et al. 2010). CRT's emphasis on the advocacy for issues of 'race,' not superiority in a hierarchy of oppressions, if carefully considered can be articulated in methodologies.

Intersectionality brings with it a challenge to CRT researchers in terms of how these complex axes of oppression can be adequately conceptualised and incorporated into methodologies, asking new questions that in many cases cannot be explored using conventional means. A CRT methodology can be identified by its attempt to include decolonised counter-narratives that question the nature of ideas whilst contributing to their development. CRT has a history, albeit recent, of presenting new voices to those more established ones as a way to counterbalance traditional perspectives and positions (see Tuhiwai Smith 2006a). In framing the Maori struggle for decolonisation, Tuhiwai Smith (2006a) describes five conditions of their struggle that could inform a CRT methodology; a critical consciousness; reimagining the world and our position within it; intersectionality; challenge to the status quo; struggle against imperialist structures. Tuhiwai Smith's approach to the Maori struggle in New Zealand offers support to an established CRT standpoint and therefore CRT methodology. However, it is also clear in this case that Maori history and reality has been deemed by Maori and other indigenous people to have been generally ignored forcing them to 'prove our own history and to prove the worth of our language and values' (Tuhiwai Smith 2006a, 156). These ideas reflect many of the realities of critical race theorists whose wish to privilege voices ignored in research, to decolonise knowledge, have found it necessary to engage in activist scholarship to transform these conditions.

From the benign to the malevolent: Everyday CRT agendas

In relation to prevalent, everyday or majoritarian stories, the 'benign' field of sport is an example of where popular views of equality, inclusion and 'melting pot' idealism often go unchallenged in research. Black people are regularly profiled in positions of success where in many other professions, outside of entertainment, they are less likely to be so prominent. However, access to sport facilities and services are popularly deemed to be available to all and in the UK the notion of 'sport for all' is a slogan from the 1970s that is still commonly used today. Still there are contradictions; the majoritarian story of sport for all is one that consistently denies racialised power relations for more commonly held neutral pluralistic discourses. When examined further these myths can be exploded, whilst research on the pluralist notions of unfettered progression for all cannot be evidenced in the scarce ethnic monitoring in governing bodies of sport and sports councils. The majoritarian view is that if there is one area of society that does not need a critical race critique it is sport. A CRT agenda would seek to challenge such views. Because sport is such a major cultural commodity to implicate it in racialised practices is to speak with certain volume about its prevalence in less commonly viewed 'equitable' and 'fair' arenas. Where research methodologies in sport (of all things) begin to explore its location in the perpetuation of racial processes and formations then they must also be commentating on, and implicating, a society stratified along lines of 'race.' Gloria Ladson-Billings (1998) question 'Just what is Critical Race Theory and what's it doing in a nice field like education?' is a question being adapted for many more arenas.

As a topic and symbol of majoritarian obfuscation, sport, like education, law, social and community services, crime, health and any other number of public arenas must not go unquestioned. My research into local government sport revealed policies and practice that were colour-blind, conceptually confused and contradictory (Hylton 2003). There were glass ceilings, poor diversity at the highest levels of policymaking and amongst senior person- nel, which reflected racial processes and formations that reinforced whiteness and the privileges that goes with it. The counterstory was one of black practitioners isolated in local government and with more influence in a voluntary pressure group outside of their councils, funding agents distrust- ful of black organisations whilst more established organisations received continued funding based upon *merit*. Merit meaning that criteria had been met in an 'objective,' 'detached' but not transparent way. Colour-blindness is a problem even in sport that reinforces oppression, racial inequality and power relations and therefore an ideal setting for a CRT critique and research. Due to racialisation, widespread institutional racism and racial for- mations in multiple settings, CRT agendas are not likely to be exhausted in this regard.

Transnational CRT?

As with most new critical perspectives there is often an element of concep- tual jousting, exploration and clarification that still occurs in the US but has typified much of the work in the UK. As CRT has become established as a robust approach to social theorizing and practice in the UK the call for praxis has become stronger (Gillborn 2011). In the US there have been many authors that have written in a celebratory way about a decade of CRT activity in education, or twenty plus years of concerted CRT activity else- where (Lynn and Parker 2006; Dixson and Rousseau 2006). In the UK our celebrations are currently about more recent milestone publications from British-based CRT scholars after our first international CRT conference (Hylton et al. 2011). CRT in the UK and US clearly have different histories and therefore any reflections on CRT research agendas become awkward just because one is more established than the other. However, Guinier and Tor- res' (2002) view that achieving racial justice and a healthy democratic process is a distinctly American challenge is not strictly accurate. Guinier and Torres outline a research agenda that is not purely American but one that overarches more specific sociocultural historical issues and events that can differentiate east from west, UK from US. While we must acknowledge our shared past and present, in a postmodern globalised world that rapidly emphasises racialised hegemony and the intersecting politics of 'race,' it is not surprising that CRT is being applied in the UK as in the US and else-where.

Walk the walk…but how far will you go?

In addition to conventional research methods, many writers have considered the use of participatory techniques for research purposes in the social sciences. These studies have ranged from ethnographies to assist pedagogy, to writing that has informed the mainstream understanding of the Asian experience of football (cf. Burdsey 2004). Critical ethnographic methods would not be out of place in a CRT methodology, where they enable a reworking of mainstream views on matters to do with 'race' they move from thick description to critical interpretation. These two positions are of equal value in the way CRT has utilised description and critical analysis to juxta-pose the everyday with more insightful accounts. The interplay of these accounts for Thomas (1993) present opportunities to prick public awareness of the everyday by offering more thought provoking emancipatory accounts. In this regard, the narrative, chronicles, and storytelling techniques men-tioned earlier in this article have been associated with CRT especially where the black experience has been so misunderstood or ignored that 'hearing' these voices becomes a powerful approach in itself. Chronicles have been popular in CRT as they generally involve accounts that make what Carter (2003) argues the implicit explicit and eschew pseudo-objectivity and neu-trality, and often with a twist. The twist occurring as description followed by critique enable alternative readings of the everyday which become as profound as 'seeing the wood for the trees' or in some cases 'fish seeing water.' For example, Matsuda's stories of reflection and action in her cam-paigns against racist speech acts have empowered lay and professional audi-ences by giving them confidence from not feeling isolated and alone (Matsuda et al. 1993, 12). Montoya's (2002, 243) use of narrative enables *namely discursive subversions, identify formation, and healing and transfor-mation…* This also occurs with Duncan (2006, 201) who emphasised the ability of stories to allow others to get into the mindset, or see the world through the eyes of those who are oppressed or subjugated. Gillborn (2009) does this through his use of fictional chronicles based on everyday proble-matics in education. Gillborn's technique, popular in CRT, allows him to sketch out and critique racial processes, thus melding a range of experiences and ideas to forge an anti-racist praxis.

Blaisdell's use of an ethnographic approach, termed 'performance ethnography' (Denzin 2003), enabled him to explore the way white teachers resist or ignore colour-blindness, white privilege and racial hierarchies. Approaches such as these can:

> Engender a methodological environment in which the researcher and the researched co-construct meaning instead of relying upon processes that dictate analysis and interpretation. (Carter 2003, 32)

Similarly, the focus of Blaisdell's conversations with teachers was used to explore liberal notions of education while using the dialogue with them to discuss more critical and therefore political approaches to teaching and learning. His understanding of knowledge as a consequence of racialised processes meant that he used his research to: (a) inform narrow traditional agendas and views in the sociology of education; and (b) try to transform liberal practitioner views for more radical ones. Kivel et al. (2009, 474) used a similar technique in a critical race ethnography, a merger of ideas from CRT and ethnography, to challenge wider racialised structural issues. They encourage researchers to move from 'describing and presenting "different experiences"...to...grounding those experiences within broader social, cultural discourses of institutional oppression.' Though the key for Blaisdell is how we can use it to **not only raise issues in relation to anti-racism** but from the point of view of praxis, how research can **actively challenge racism** amongst teachers. For Blaisdell the challenge is to see how we can move on from the 'objective,' 'detached' researcher that, in revealing new insights, does not take the opportunity to develop 'effective analytical techniques' to directly challenge social relations. By not explicitly challenging these social relations are researchers being complicit in perpetuating the very behaviours they seek to disrupt? Do they absolve themselves of challenging racism, or are these strategic issues in researching 'race' for transformation? (Blaisdell 2009, 1–3). How far to walk the walk...stick or twist?

Ladson-Billings and Donnor (2008), and Blaisdell (2009) emphasise this problematic for CRT scholars when they urge scholars not to over-rely on others to take their ideas forward and to promote this activism themselves. Their ultimate point is that CRT's emphasis on social justice and transformation cannot hope that the very people, privileged by racial inequalities are going to be the ones to energise these agendas and change behaviours. In this regard they both make salient points, Blaisdell (2009, 110) states that:

> If qualitative researchers rely on other people using their findings to do the work of combating racism...the assumption is that those findings will push the antiracist agenda along [but] ...they may potentially perpetuate the adherence to problematic racial views of their participants [or readers]. (Blaisdell 2009, 110).

And Ladson-Billings and Donnor (2008, 74) posit that:

> Scholars who take on the challenge of moral and ethical work cannot rely solely on others to make sense of their work and translate it into usable form.

The empowering of the excluded Other in the transformation of racialised arrangements is a core goal of Pizarro's research for social justice. Pizarro's constant tension in the way he conducted his earlier ethnographic studies was that he felt as though he was still filtering the voice of the subjects as the teller of the story and was conscious of the hypocrisy of these actions. Empowering new voices involves a 'buy-in' to research that speaks to them too by offering the promise/potential for them to influence change. Without this connection then participatory transformation is unlikely. Researchers using CRT may engage in Freirian dialogue, as illustrated by Pizarro (1999), with the subjects contributing to the study, especially where their education has systematically reduced their confidence to offer authoritative views on their social contexts because *experts don't look like them nor come from where they do...do they?* Though his methodology was innovative, in comparison to more traditional methods, and also because the study included new subjects for research in education, the process of analysis still excluded them. He wanted to include Chicano/a students in the process of the telling of their experiences *and* analysis of what was important. Therefore, Pizarro (Pizarro 1999, 58) felt it necessary to make his CRT research identifiable by framing it as research *on* empowerment and research *as* empowerment. Flores and Garcia (2009) would argue that a participatory approach that draws upon a CRF and Lat/Crit epistemology could establish the conditions for a transformation of people and individuals, though this takes much reflexivity and understanding of complex processes. This intellectual and grassroots challenge is highlighted by Stovall (2006) in his struggles with (and for) community organizations, secondary schools and the academy. Stovall's documenting of his participation in, and reflection on, community interactions with the establishment, in the development of new education facilities, illustrates some of the difficulties that Pizarro found in adopting a participatory transformative agenda. The need for 'actions following words' is the focus of work by other CRT authors (see also Parker and Stovall 2004).

Summary

Carspecken (1996) and Christians (2007) summarise principles attractive to CRT researchers. For instance, Carspecken states the major element of social research is its political engagement making it more likely to make a difference to mainstream agendas. He argues that, critical researchers should be engaged in social and cultural criticism, that there should be recognition of inequality in society, that oppressive dominant forces should be laid bare and challenged, that oppression has to be tackled on more than one front, that mainstream epistemologies, and research agendas, make up part of the forces of oppression. Research that falls into this category is similar to that of Christians (2007), whose work explores the ethics of resistance in social science. Research that allows us to understand everyday realities and challenges the value neutral, apolitical positivism that is *de rigeur* in many research circles:

> ...the challenge for those writing culture is not to limit their moral perspectives to their own generic and neutral principles, but to engage the same moral space as the people they study...research strategies are not assessed...in terms of 'experimental robustness' but...'vitality and vigour in illuminating how we can create human flourishing.' (Christians 2007, 57)

The notion that the personal, professional and political should be tied into methodological processes is one that supports a major thrust of enlightened meaningful critical research. Such a shift is one that is not taken lightly but one that engages the researcher in a process of identification with the subject that leaves the reader in no doubt that a political position has been taken within the framework of ethical knowledge generation and social transformation. The researcher's ability to exacerbate power differentials even in critical research can be alleviated when CRT centres the subject, and ensures that research is *for*, rather than *on*, the subjects in question, and the researcher is located within the study (Bhopal 2000). The reflexivity necessary for a researcher to 'enter' the research and adopt a political stance towards their study enables them to examine and question the differences and similarities which exist between the researcher and the researched and how this affects access, the influence of personal experience and power (Bhopal 2000, 70). A CRT technique is identifiable in Bhopal's work due to her use of intersectionality in recognising the overlaying of social factors on social relations both inside and outside of research. Intersectionality, racialised power processes, and reflexivity are core organising CRT concepts underpinned by emancipatory politics.

No trite answer is offered to the question '*what is a CRT methodology?*' because that in itself would reflect a pedantic essentialism anathema to critical race theorists. A CRT methodology must embrace not only the spirit of CRT but practical liberatory, transformative elements. The *spirit of CRT* is a useful notion here because CRT is not theoretically abstract, nor dogmatically defined, neither is it for armchair theorists. For example, Matsuda et al. (1993) would describe a CRT methodology as one that is grounded in the experience of our collective realities. More specifically, a CRT methodology should demonstrate a response to challenging subordination and oppression...*it is informed by active struggle and in turn informs that struggle* (Matsuda et al. 1993). These are principles that can guide any combination of research techniques from the traditional to more challenging cutting edge methods. So just as CRT methodologies can facilitate knowledge of racialised relations and activism to transform them and other forms of oppression, if poorly considered they can also stymie these activities (Tuhiwai Smith 2006b).

Where a CRT framework is only partially applied in theory rather than practice then critical researchers could be accused of *talking the talk, but not walking the walk*. Researching racialised problematics ultimately leads scholars to a point where they must agitate for change and unfortunately be willing to defend positions that are marginal, challenging and sometimes plain unpopular. All things considered there is no positive spin on 'race' and racism because 'race' is a construct that is used to differentiate, (dis) advantage, and (dis)empower each time it is uncritically invoked. Even positive social transformation will involve remarking upon these racialised concepts and processes and to this end, simply, involves telling someone something about themselves/the world that needs to change.

Key considerations for CRT that emerge from the work of CRT researchers like Blaisdell, Ladson-Billings, Kivel et al. is how CRT methodologies can not only shift from making important theoretical and conceptual contributions that disrupt racial processes but also how they can challenge them directly. In many cases CRT methodologies force researchers to contradict what is often viewed as sound ethical practice[3] through encouraging a more central positioning in the research process; 'researchers as part of the process, in practice, look like this.' Some researchers will have to fight their natural urges, based upon years of training where they have been constantly told to locate themselves outside of the research process, to now locate themselves, as social beings, inside the research process. Dialogue with researchers, far from leading the respondents, retains elements of heuristics, and dialogic performance that encourages an inclusive and participative approach.

- The 'spirit' of CRT
- No methods are inherently CRT though some have more utility than others
- Social justice focus
- A challenge to oppression and subordination
- Strategic challenge to racism/challenge convention
- Centre the black voice/black experience
- Research is for, not on, the subjects in question
- Conceptually strategic/pragmatic/anti-essentialist
- Intersectionality: strategic incorporation of class, gender, sexuality and other oppressive social categories, however they are less likely to be foregrounded in the first instance.
- Counter-storytelling
- Praxis oriented
- Activist scholarship
- Participatory approach
- Researcher as part of the process
- Challenges the passive reproduction of established questions and practices

Figure 1. Key considerations for Critical Race Theory methodologies.

CRT methodologies are focused on philosophical and ethical imperatives that explore, confront and change negative racialised relations. They may also be identifiable by their willingness to challenge the fundamental basis of CRT's key categories. 'Race,' ethnicity, racism and related issues of anti-racism, identities, and intersectionality are arbitrary and laden with 'everyday' ambiguities. An acceptance of the pervasiveness of racism and racialisation in society is not necessarily an acceptance of the notion of 'race' and its related social categories. CRT methodologies must navigate the topography of racialised language in a way that is unambiguous because 'race' is a paradox in that we know it is socially constructed, changes over time, and has no scientific basis. CRT researchers must then be wary of these ambiguities in light of the 'reality' of 'race' in the vernacular and our everyday lives.

Figure 1 emphasises some of the key considerations for researchers using a CRT methodology. They are in no particular order but are points and issues that must be balanced in a rationale underpinning a CRT methodology. This list is not exhaustive but indicative of the way key ideas from CRT need to pervade a discussion of methodology. A methodology is the point at which theory and practice merge and so the defence of a story of how CRT underpins the practical aspects of a research study must be cognisant of this delicate balance. Parker et al. (1999, 27) offer a message of solidarity with those adopting a CRT methodology:

> Adopting and adapting CRT as a framework [...] means that we will have to expose racism [...] *and* propose radical solutions for addressing it. We may have to defend a radical approach to democracy that seriously undermines the privilege of those who have so skilfully carved that privilege into the foundation of the nation.

CRT methodologies should be identifiable by their innovation in the methods that they use to explore social relations and racialised problematics. However, CRT research methods are ostensibly tools available for use in any social investigation so there must be other checks and balances for a methodology using such a framework in a plethora of settings and contexts. For example, Parker et al. (1999) emphasise a critical race consciousness to guard against ahistorical approaches to research; Glover (2009) emphasises asking new questions in approaches to researching 'race'; Blaisdell (2009) and others like Ladson-Billings and Donnor (2008) encourage a researcher–activist approach; others encourage an empowering participatory one (Denzin 2003; Pizarro 1999; Stovall 2006). Pizarro (1999) emphasises the participatory and transformative element of research, arguing that there must be discernible social justice measures to establish the strength, or relative worth of research. Philosophically, Pizarro's ideas have much support within CRT and those conducting critical research, though the significance of the kinds of change and transformation are also interesting and pressing questions for further deliberation. Suffice it to say that CRT methodologies can engender transformative capacity. Yet how attractive they become to new generations of researchers starts with a consistent and persuasive defence of this potential.

Notes

1. It is worth noting here that CRT is a theoretical framework rather than 'a theory.'
2. Even as well respected members of their academic/local communities they realise that there will be regular moments that remind them of their racialised status in society.
3. Due to conventional ethical guidelines relating to detached, objective and neutral researcher.

References

Bhopal, K. 2000. Gender, "race" and power in the research process. In *Research and inequality*, ed. C. Truman, D.M. Mertens, and B. Humphries, 67–79. London: UCL Press.

Blaisdell, B. 2009. *Seeing with poetic eyes: Critical race theory and moving from liberal to critical forms of race research in the sociology of education*. Rotterdam: Sense Publishers.

Bulmer, M., and J. Solomos, eds. 2004. *Researching race and racism*. London: Routledge.

Burdsey, D.C. 2004. From Brick Lane to White Hart Lane? Football, anti-racism and young, male, British Asian identities. Uxbridge: Brunel University: 1 v.

Burdsey, D.C. 2011. Applying a CRT lens to sport in the UK: The case of professional football. In *Atlantic crossings: International dialogues on critical race theory*, ed. K. Hylton, A. Pilkington, P. Warmington, and S. Housee, 39–60. Birmingham: CSAP/Higher Education Academy.

Carspecken, P. 1996. *Critical ethnography: A practical guide*. London: Routledge.

Carter, M. 2003. Telling tales out of school: "What's the fate of a black story in a white world of white stories?" In *Interrogating racism in qualitative research methodology*, ed. G. Lopez and L. Parker, 29–48. New York: Peter Lang.

Chakrabarty, N. 2011. *If I were white...*From Beyoncé's imaginings to the age of Obama. In *Atlantic crossings: International dialogues on critical race theory*, ed. K. Hylton, A. Pilkington, P. Warmington, and S. Housee, 208–22. Birmingham: CSAP/Higher Education Academy.

Christians, C. 2007. Neutral science and the ethics of resistance. In *Ethical futures in qualitative research: Decolonizing the politics of knowledge*, ed. N. Denzin and M. Giardina, 47–66. Walnut Creek, CA: Left Coast Press.

Cole, M. 2009. *Critical race theory and education: A Marxist response*. Basingstoke: Palgrave Macmillan.

Cole, M. 2011. The CRT concept of 'white supremacy' as applied to the UK: Eight major problematics and some educational implication. In *Atlantic crossings: International dialogues on critical race theory*, ed. K. Hylton, A. Pilkington, P. Warmington, and S. Housee, 244–65. Birmingham: CSAP/Higher Education Academy.

Collins, P. 1990. *Black feminist thought*. London: Routledge.

Crenshaw, K. 1995. Mapping the margins: Intersectionality, identity politics, and violence against women of color. In *Critical race theory: The key writings that informed the movement*, ed. K. Crenshaw, N. Gotanda, G. Peller, and K. Thomas, 357–83. New York: The New Press.

Crenshaw, K., N. Gotanda, G. Peller, and K. Thomas, eds. 1995. *Critical race theory: The key writings that formed the movement*. New York: New Press.

Delgado Bernal, D. 2002. Critical race theory, Latino critical theory, and critical raced-gendered epistemologies: Recognizing students of color as holders and creators of knowledge. *Qualitative Inquiry* 8, no. 1: 105–26.

Delgado, R., and J. Stefancic. 1999. *Critical race theory: The cutting edge*. Philadelphia, PA: Temple University Press.

Denzin, N.K. 2003. *Performance ethnography: Critical pedagogy and the politics of culture*. Thousand Oaks, CA and London: Sage.

Denzin, N.K., and M.D. Giardina. 2006. *Qualitative inquiry and the conservative challenge*. Walnut Creek, CA: Left Coast.

Denzin, N.K., and M.D. Giardina. 2007. *Ethical futures in qualitative research: Decolonizing the politics of knowledge*. Walnut Creek, CA: Left Coast Press.

Denzin, N.K., Y. Lincoln, and L. Tuhiwai Smith, eds. 2008. *Handbook of critical and indigenous methodologies*. London: Sage.

Dixson, A.D., and C.K. Rousseau. 2006. *Critical race theory in education: All God's children got a song*. New York and London: Routledge.

Dockery, G. 2000. Participatory research: Whose role whose responsibility? In *Research and inequality*, ed. C. Truman, D.M. Mertens, and B. Humphries, 95–110. London: UCL.

Dunbar, C. 2008. Critical race theory and indigenous methodologies. In *Handbook of critical and indigenous methodologies*, ed. N.N. Denzin, Y. Lincoln, and L. Tuhiwai Smith, 85–99. London: Sage.

Duncan, G.A. 2006. Critical race ethnography in education: Narrative, inequality, and the problem of epistemology. In *Critical race theory in education: All God's children got a song*, ed. A.D. Dixson and C.K. Rousseau, 191–212. London: Routledge.

Flores, J., and S. Garcia. 2009. Latina testimonios: A reflexive, critical analysis of a 'Latina space' at a predominantly white campus. *Race Ethnicity and Education* 12, no. 2: 155–72.

Gillborn, D. 2005. Education policy as an act of white supremacy: Whiteness, critical race theory and education reform. *Journal of Education Policy* 20, no. 4: 485–505.

Gillborn, D. 2006. Critical race theory and education: Racism and anti-racism in educational theory and praxis. *Discourse: Studies in the Cultural Politics of Education* 27, no. 1: 11–32.

Gillborn, D. 2008. Coincidence or conspiracy? Whiteness, policy and the persistence of the Black/White achievement gap. *Educational Review* 60, no. 3: 229–48.

Gillborn, D. 2009. *Racism and education: Coincidence or conspiracy?* London: Routledge.

Gillborn, D. 2011. Once upon a time in the UK: Race, class, hope and Whiteness in the academy: Personal reflections on the birth of 'Britcrit'. In *Atlantic crossings: International dialogues on critical race theory*, ed. K. Hylton, A. Pilkington, P. Warmington, and S. Housee, 21–38. Birmingham: CSAP.

Glover, K. 2009. *Racial profiling: Research, racism and resistance*. Plymouth: Rowman & Littlefield Publishers.

Goldberg, D. 1993. *Racist culture*. Oxford: Blackwell.

Guinier, L., and G. Torres. 2002. *The miner's canary: Enlisting race, resisting power, transforming democracy*. Cambridge: Harvard University Press.

Gunaratnam, Y. 2003. *Researching 'race' and ethnicity: Methods, knowledge and power*. London: Sage.

Hankivsky, H., and A. Christoffersen. 2008. Intersectionality and the determinants of health: A Canadian perspective. *Critical Public Health* 18, no. 3: 271–83.

Hankivsky, H., C. Reid, et al. 2010. Exploring the promises of intersectionality for advancing women's health research. *International Journal for Equity in Health* 9, no. 5: 1–15.

Harvey, L. 1990. *Critical social research*. London: Unwin-Hyman.

Hermes, M. 1999. Toward a first nations methodology. In *Race is...race isn't*, ed. L. Parker, D. Deyhle, and S. Villenas, 83–100. Colorado: Westview Press.

Hylton, K. 2003. *Local government, 'race' and sports policy implementation: Demystifying equal opportunities in local government*. Leeds: Leeds Metropolitan University: 1 v.

Hylton, K. 2005. "Race", sport and leisure: Lessons from critical race theory. *Leisure Studies* 24, no. 1: 81–98.

Hylton, K. 2009. *'Race' and sport: Critical race theory*. London: Routledge.

Hylton, K., A. Pilkington, P. Warmington, and S. Housee, eds. 2011. *Atlantic crossings: International dialogues on critical race theory*. Birmingham: CSAP/Higher Education Academy.

Housee, S. 2008. Should ethnicity matter when teaching about 'race' and racism in the classroom? *Race Ethnicity and Education* 11, no. 4: 415–28.

Kivel, B.D., C.W. Johnson, and S. Scraton. 2009. (Re)Theorizing leisure experience and race. *Journal of Leisure Research* 41, no. 4: 473–93.

Knaus, C. 2009. Shut up and listen: Applied critical race theory in the classroom. *Race, Ethnicity and Education* 12, no. 2: 133–54.

Ladson-Billings, G. 1998. Just what is critical race theory and what's it doing in a nice field like education? *Qualitative Studies in Education* 1, no. 11: 7–24.

Ladson-Billings, G., and J. Donnor. 2008. Waiting for the call: The moral activist role of critical race theory scholarship. In *Handbook of critical and indigenous methodologies*, ed. N. Denzin, Y. Lincoln, and L. Tuhiwai Smith, 61–83. London: Sage.

Lopez, G., and L. Parker, eds. 2003. *Interrogating racism in qualitative research methodology*. New York: Peter Lang.

Ludvig, A. 2006. Differences between women? Intersecting voices in a female narrative. *European Journal of Women's Studies* 13, no. 3: 245–8.

Lynn, M., and L. Parker. 2006. Critical race studies in education: Examining a decade of research on U.S. schools. *The Urban Review* 38, no. 4: 257–90.

Matsuda, M.J., C.R. Lawrence, R. Delgado, and K.W. Crenshaw. 1993. *Words that wound: Critical race theory assaultive speech, and the First Amendment*. Boulder, CO: Westview Press.

Montoya, M.E. 2002. Celebrating racialized legal narratives. In *Crossroads directions and a new critical race theory*, ed. F. Valdes, J.M. Culp, and A.P. Harris. Philadelphia, PA: Temple University Press.

Parker, L., D. Deyhle, and S. Villenas, eds. 1999. *Race is...race isn't: Critical race theory and qualitative studies in education*. Boulder, CO: Westview Press.

Parker, L., and D. Stovall. 2004. Actions following words: Critical race theory connects to critical pedagogy. *Educational Philosophy and Theory* 36, no. 2: 167–82.

Phoenix, A., and P. Pattynama. 2006. Intersectionality. *European Journal of Women's Studies* 13, no. 3: 187–92.

Pilkington, A. 2011. 'Business as usual': Racial inequality in the Academy ten years after Macpherson. In *Atlantic crossings: International dialogues on critical race theory*, ed. K. Hylton, A. Pilkington, P. Warmington, and S. Housee. Birmingham: CSAP/Higher Education Academy.

Pizarro, M. 1999. "Adelante": Toward social justice and empowerment in Chicana/o communities and Chicana/o studies? In *Race is... race isn't: Critical race theory and qualitative studies in education*, ed. L. Parker, D. Deyhle, and S. Villenas, 53–82. Boulder, CO: Westview Press.

Preston, J. 2008. Protect and survive: 'Whiteness' and the middle-class family in civil defence pedagogies. *Journal of Education Policy* 23, no. 5: 469–82.

Seidman, S. 2004. *Contested knowledge: Social theory today.* Blackwell: Oxford.

Solorzano, D., and T. Yosso. 2002. Critical race methodology: Counterstorytelling as an analytical framework for educational research. *Qualitative Inquiry* 8, no. 1: 23–44.

Song, M. 2004. Introduction: Who's at the bottom? Examining claims about racial hierarchy. *Ethnic and Racial Studies* 27, no. 6: 859–77.

Song, M. 2010. Is there 'a' mixed race group in Britain? The diversity of multiracial identification and experience. *Critical Social Policy* 30, no. 3: 337–58.

Stovall, D. 2006. Forging community in race and class: Critical race theory and the quest for social justice in education. *Race Ethnicity and Education* 9, no. 3: 243–59.

Thomas, J. 1993. *Doing critical ethnography.* London: Sage.

Tuhiwai Smith, L. 2006a. Choosing the margins: The role of research in indigenous struggles for social justice. In *Qualitative inquiry and the conservative challenge*, ed. N.G. Denzin and M. Giardina. London: Left Coast Press.

Tuhiwai Smith, L. 2006b. *Decolonizing methodologies: Research and indigenous people.* London: Zed Books.

Tweed, T. 2006. *Crossing and dwelling: A theory of religion.* London: Harvard University Press.

Tyson, C. 2003. Epistemology of emancipation. In *Interrogating racism in qualitative research*, ed. G. Lopez and L. Parker, 19–28. New York: Peter Lang.

Warmington, P. 2011. Some of my best friends are Marxists: CRT sociocultural theory and the 'figured worlds' of race. In *Atlantic crossings: International dialogues on critical race theory*, ed. K. Hylton, A. Pilkington, P. Warmington, and S. Housee, 266–86. Birmingham: CSAP/Higher Education Academy.

Buried alive: the psychoanalysis of racial absence in preparedness/education

Namita Chakrabarty

Based on extracts from an ethnography produced during the ESRC 2009–10 research project, *'Preparedness Pedagogies' and Race: An Interdisciplinary Approach*, this article explores the racialized culture of civil defence in the UK whilst also critiquing the world of higher education. The ethnographic artefacts of interviews, observations of preparedness role play around fictional character, and of professionals' live reminiscence of emergency, are explored through the lens of the psychoanalytical construction of being *buried alive*; Critical Race Theory (CRT) conceptions of policy constitution of a social world that imprisons the non-white citizen and the other are seen, in this article, as enshrined in this construction. Freud's *The Uncanny* encompasses the psychology of being 'buried alive,' and one conception of this is seen as a state akin to life in the womb, a strange place of safety. In contrast I use two CRT narratives of resilience auto-education as a way of beginning to analyse different presentations of being *buried alive*. I refer, following Royle, to Edgar Allan Poe's *The Premature Burial* and his introductory conception of being *buried alive* as being something that happens to others, about the affective act of burial; in contrast I draw on the chapter entitled 'Buried Alive,' in the sensation novel *Lady Audley's Secret*, a useful metaphor for the eternal live imprisonment of the other facilitated by legal means, ensuring the security of a racially pure, class secure, hetero-normative status quo: the burial of race. This burial within policy is double edged: the shadow character *buried alive* within preparedness and within education haunts the work and is thus more likely to return as evoked by the events of 9/11.

Background

The title of this article, *'Buried alive*: the psychoanalysis of racial absence in preparedness/education,' emerged from an ESRC funded study[1] 'Preparedness Pedagogies, and Race,' carried out in the UK during 2009–10. The study analysed traces of 'race,' buried within civil defence performative exercise:

these are event type exercises where preparedness professionals practice how they will deal with emergencies and disasters, to protect citizens, via fictional scenarios. The research involved three methods: firstly, interviews were carried out with 20 professionals working within UK preparedness; secondly, focus groups were held with members of the public to explore reaction to public information booklets; thirdly, observations were carried out of five preparedness exercises organised by governmental and commercial organisations in 2009 in the UK. The five sites of preparedness exercises ranged from a nuclear bunker to airport facilities, and the themes addressed included swine flu and aviation accident preparedness. A range of personnel were involved including police, fire, ambulance and airport staff, besides volunteers acting as survivors and victims. The ethnographer observed the professional staff involved, but was also a participant within some of the exercises. The ethnographic data was collected via photography, video recording, and written notes of the observations. Observation was directed towards scene, character and setting. Ethical consideration was observed within the methodologies; no individuals were named or shown in the ensuing material. A performance ethnography was produced to document the results emerging from the study, this became *Emergency Exercise 2010: Operation Snowman*, a youth drama event, performing a tabletop exercise, held, *buried alive*, in a nuclear bunker.

The latter description of the research process frames the project in the third person, and in the neutral un-biased terms of academia, however the project proposal emphasised its use of CRT in order to focus on the presence of race in the study, and one of the key techniques of CRT is its use of counter-narrative; in this sense CRT makes visible the words and thoughts that may hitherto have been absent in academic texts, the 'I,' or eye, of the absent personalised voice.

From third person to first: the counter-narrative of the research process

I was the sole investigator on the observation of preparedness exercises during the project, and the term *buried alive* hovered in my mind through out the whole research project so much so that I started a file, entitled 'buried alive: thoughts on ethnography,' early on in the project. This became a journal of reflections on what I observed in the field of preparedness, about the characters and sites. The journal also documented the uncanny similarities between the work of emergency planning professionals performing resilience[2] education, and that of educationalists, performing the work of higher education. The journal also tracked my shadow thoughts on research and life, and on the work of the black minority ethnic (BME) academic researcher within fields inhabited by whiteness. The ESRC team was made up of three researchers, two white and myself – the one BME researcher on the project. As I was predominantly working alone in the field of observation my research colleagues were replaced by the preparedness professionals encountered during the observation of exercises. Inevitably I had an uneasy relationship with the latter as they were aware that I was observing them within the exercises, but also, within a UK preparedness culture that is predominantly white, my race felt like a wall of skin between us.

I began to feel further and further divorced from the research team when we met or communicated. It felt as if I was experiencing and interpreting the culture of preparedness in a different way from the white researchers who saw 'covert racism' as 'unusual' and the study demonstrated the '"unreliability" of "white" narratives' (Preston et al. 2010, 8), even those using CRT as a means of interpretation. Thus within the preparedness observation, but also within the educational research experience, I increasingly felt *buried alive*. I realised that the duality of my feelings about preparedness and education resides in the word resilience, and this echoed somewhere deep inside of me, about my experience as a BME citizen in the UK, but also as a BME professional in education in a time of diversity. It was as if I was underneath 'a brick wall' (Ahmed 2009, 48) which had fallen down on top of me; I could see the light outside and hear voices above, but I couldn't shove aside or lift the debris that had fallen on top of me – the building bricks of racism: the structures that keep whiteness alive and race dead; like a victim of an earthquake I found myself, *buried alive*.

The interests of this article lie within the psychological experience of being *buried alive* as raced experience, along side questions of the role of race within UK preparedness, and in education; shadowing this is the unacknowledged preparedness involved in being raced – a work of BME resilience ongoing and generally unacknowledged. With this in mind the article starts with an introduction and two CRT counter-narratives as a means of defining the concept of race and being *buried alive* within preparedness experience and within education; the research questions and methodology are then detailed; the research findings are analysed and conclusions are drawn in relation to preparedness and education as epitomised in cultural policy since 9/11.

Introductory counter-narrative, since 9/11

Figure 1 The image shows the remnants of 9/11 and the actuality of being *buried alive*: mourners haunt Ground Zero trying to imagine the horror and terror of being *buried alive*; tourists and academics take photos from across the other side of the road: I see beside the criss-cross of rebuilding on top of what is buried below, the symbolic white 'one way' sign and next to it a 'side walk closed' sign too – the symbolism of the racial divide interrogated by Obama's 'yes, we can,' echoing across the Middle East now in 2011. But here at Ground Zero there is an almost absence of race now, it's just an urban sprawl, although the event, unleashed by a clash of cultures, has become the catalyst for the battleground of race. The image shows the uncanny web of preparedness and of culture, that some mourn and look for

Figure 1.   Outside Ground Zero (Chakrabarty 2010).

meaning, others regroup for resilience, and prepare for something worse: the sign to 'Brooklyn Bridge' and the street named after the church indicate the uncanny duality of our response to raced terror.

Buried alive, a metaphor for racial resilience auto-education: two CRT counter-narratives

Everyday battles

1. One day at work at the university, a BME academic was in a shared tutorial space meeting room off a corridor opposite the student reception desk. Over the afternoon alongside other staff meeting their students she met with her students, one to one at timed intervals. There was nothing out of the ordinary about that day, other than that she was wearing a 24 hour heart monitor, as requested by her consultant. A heart monitor is worn hanging around the neck, under the clothes; it records changes to the heart rhythm. Alongside the monitor the patient is asked to keep a written record of anything in particular that is felt, during the 24 hours. The dual records then aid the consultant in diagnosing the heart problem, and medication or treatment is then provided to extend the patient's resilience to their heart condition.

On this particular day, apart from the cumbersome nature of having the monitor hanging against her chest under her clothes, everything felt normal. The tutorials finished, the academic left the room through the door that had been open all afternoon, and walked a few steps down the corridor, approaching the reception desk. The white male administrative assistant sitting at the desk said:

Oh, hi...I thought you weren't here, I've just emailed Edward[3] [her white, male line manager] to say you're not here!

Her heart jumped and started to pound so loudly that she felt her heart would leap through her skin. Her pulse pounding she started to feel as if the ceiling and walls were coming closer, as though they were going to *bury her alive*. She said:

Why did you do that? I've been here all afternoon, in the room I'm supposed to be in – look here, right opposite.

He explained that a student had said that the academic wasn't in the tutorial room, perhaps they had looked in the wrong room, or not far enough into the room which was crowded with staff and students, and so the student had reported to the administrative assistant that the academic was absent; he in turn had emailed her line manager to report her absence. She said:

But I've been here all this time, in the room that I'm supposed to be in, the one advertised on the timetable.

She asked the administrative assistant to re-email the line manager and explain that she was present, not absent.

Later she checked her email: the administrative assistant had sent the email and an apology. By then she was at home and her heart had calmed down; on her 24 hour written record for her consultant she wrote up the heart pounding experience from earlier and her feeling of being *buried alive*; under location and activity she put 'at work, stressful work conversation.'

In the morning she went to the hospital and had the monitor removed, but as she reached home the phone rang. It was the hospital; uncannily around about the time her heart felt as if it was trying to jump through her skin, when her physical presence was being *buried alive*, the monitor had stopped.

Some months later, at her staff review, the incident came up. Her line manager brought up the original email from the administrative assistant; he seemed unable to remove the white administrative assistant's labelling of her presence as absence, despite her protests, and despite the second email from the assistant attempting to delete the first.

The white male word of absence of race was stronger than the live presence of BME race. She became a premature ghost, a headless body without a voice, her heart stopped, she was dismembered into an invisible body involved in work, *buried alive* by the words of a white professional naming her absence.

'The word racism is very sticky' (Ahmed 2009, 47), so she does not allude to what this is that she's stuck within, but the stain of skin is even stickier than words like 'racism' and 'absence'; white conception of skin is inescapable and dooms race; by inverting hierarchies, and language, the work space is a white space, BME staff are *buried alive*.

7/7

2. On the 7th July 2005 I was at home getting ready to go to Heathrow to catch a flight to Spain on a research trip when I started to hear non-stop sirens outside. I went online, central London had been hit by four suicide bombers.[4] As the day went on the sirens continued, and outside my flat there were lots of travellers standing with their luggage looking lost and stranded as the entire transport network was closed down. On the radio there were announcements to stay away from public buildings and not to travel unless necessary; this was an uncanny instruction for me as at that point I lived next to a major tourist site and I could see from the window the police setting up to cordon it off, so I repacked taking only what I could comfortably carry and headed off downstairs, with my British passport, to catch a cab to the airport.

Outside Waterloo station the queue for taxis went down the length of the building and then curled back on itself. There were very few taxis. The atmosphere was tense. I decided to be proactive and community minded, and I was also determined to get to the airport, so I called out as I walked down the queue:

Anyone going to Heathrow, want to share the cost of a taxi?'
A young woman, with an Afrikaans accent called back:

Who'd want to share a cab with you?'
I said:

What do you mean?'
She said:

Have you looked in the mirror?'

For a moment, strangely, I was puzzled. What could she mean? Despite wearing casual clothes, jeans, t-shirt and a jacket, I was still dressed OK, I'd showered, combed my hair…what did she mean? I stared at her. She put me out of, and into, my misery, simultaneously.

Who'd want to share a cab with an Asian on a day like this?
Other people, hearing her words turned to stare at me too, as if I was an alien species in a cage, not a human being, a member of the same species as themselves.

I moved away, my heart beating fast, and buried inside and under my Asian skin on the first occasion of suicide bombings in London. But this moment happened before anyone knew that what came to be known as 7/7, echoing 9/11, was produced by the actions of four BME men, three of whom were Asian, who'd blown themselves up along side multicultural others. But it's what 'people' already thought, always think, BME people are guilty until proven innocent, and then they are still guilty, *buried alive*. That feeling back again. I wanted to get out of London and the UK, I didn't want to be trapped a moment longer.

Eventually I shared a cab with another raced body, a woman from Chile. We travelled together, *buried alive* in a black cab, but more resilient together. We passed police cars and vans on the motorway; young BME men and women were being taken out of their vehicles, and searched; the bonnets and boots of their cars open too like the bodies of rape victims left for dead in an inter-ethnic war.

At the airport, the army had transformed the site with guns and tanks, but we had our tickets and passports. We got out alive, for a while.

Buried alive: the theory, and some definitions

1. Buried alive – a safe womb-like place

> To some people the idea of being *buried alive by mistake* is the most uncanny thing of all. And yet psycho-analysis has taught us that this terrifying phantasy is only a transformation of another phantasy which had originally nothing terrifying about it at all.... I mean, of intra-uterine existence. (Freud 1919 [1997a], 220, emphasis added)

From outside, looking in, being *buried alive* reminds us of that primary place of safety, the womb, as shown in the writings of psychoanalysis. In preparedness and classic cold war civil defence the womb is replaced by the nuclear bunker – a safe place for the chosen in a time of crisis, a place where the carefully selected can retreat and regroup, ready for resurrection.

2. Buried alive – a mistake

As children, and then as adults, our fear of 'being buried alive by mistake' (Freud 1919 [1997a], 220) follows us through life and is played out for us on the 24 hour news channels displaying images of natural disasters or accidents, the emergencies that are prepared for by preparedness professionals, the work of resilience. In 2010 we followed the good news of the Chile miners who were *buried alive*, but ultimately survived through the work of engineering and civil defence. But we also see bad news too – the earthquakes and hurricanes around the world, Mother Earth threatening to bury us back within, inside her body.

The major news event of the first decade since the millennium was the premeditated terror of non-state organisations and their work, epitomised in the events of 9/11, and framed within the psychological metaphor of being *buried alive*. The 9/11, or 11 September 2001, attacks on the Twin Towers and on the Pentagon, are prophesied within Freud's description of the uncanny. The use of a familiar means of transport translated into a tool of death echoing the imagination of disaster entertainment (Zizek 2002, 16–17); the reversal of nationals from Eastern bombed nations, hitherto the victims of war, launching themselves the most audacious attack to bury alive the Western nation who first used the bomb on the east, burying alive Western nationals; the symbolic translated into the real:

> There is one more point. . .I think it deserves special emphasis. This is that an uncanny effect is often and easily produced when the distinction between imagination and reality is effaced, as when something that we have hitherto regarded as imaginary appears before us in reality, or when a symbol takes over the full functions of the thing it symbolises, *and so on*. (Freud 1919 [1997a], 221, emphasis added)

3. Buried alive – the everyday of 'and so on'

I am intrigued by the 'and so on,' the use of every day language for the extraordinary. Like racism, which for the victims becomes everyday – a perpetual 'and so on' that we experience and cannot catalogue constantly otherwise we'd get nothing else done. Racism is uncanny for BME people. It's there all the time. It is familiar like the outline of a human body is recognizable as a human. What is unfamiliar about racism is how illogical it is to us, BME people: we know that we are humans, because we are looking from inside our bodies, through our eyes, to the outside world; we see bodies, similar but different, just the surface difference, skin; we expect to be treated equally, for others to see past the skin, inside the body; we would wish for others to treat us as they would wish to be treated. We look as if from a safe place, like the womb, where the world is benign, protective and as one entity. However, if we look from outside, from the perspective of those who cannot see what's buried but only what's on the surface – the skin, the dying part of the human – we see that racism is also uncanny: because if the body is similar, so too is the treatment: the treatment meted out to those who resemble the perpetrators of racism but for the skin – the surface difference has to be erased for the survival of the species, otherwise the species won't know who to trust. The human body becomes untrustworthy, like a damaged limb, it must be – uncannily – severed, to become whole again.

4. Buried alive - the terminal of death

> The bodies were recovered with hands bound behind back with rope and were blindfolded. There were no signs of torture or gunshot wound, which led the IPE%%% to believe the local national(s)%%% were *buried alive*.

(Wikileaks 2010, 2006-03-14 11:15:00, brackets and emphasis added)

The literal term *buried alive* has resurfaced after being doubly *buried alive* in the lack of statistics and information of non-allied deaths in Iraq and Afghanistan; the resurrection of the word came via the website Wikileaks in its 'Warlogs' pages. The latter are fully searchable and open access, or were until early December 2010 when the website came under attack after revelations of US diplomacy contraventions under the Geneva conventions. What I found interesting in the above example from the 'Warlogs' is the absence of the uncanny in this real life example of being buried alive. I note that in writing buried alive in this instance I do not surround the phrase with the skin of italics to denote the symbolic, these deaths are premeditated and actually happened: the individuals were the intended inhabitants of the burial, the blindfolds are the weapons of war that mask the criminals and force the victim into the uncanny and real experience simultaneously – into having to imagine what it looks like to be buried alive when it is actually physically happening to them: at the abyss of human experience and human action, between humans.

Royle in his chapter entitled 'Buried Alive' directs us to Poe's 1844 short story, *The Premature Burial* (Royle 2003, 145–6); what is of interest in this article is that Poe's reading of the experience of being *buried alive* is initially seen from the outside, and is performed in the glee of the colonial voice: he says the reader gets a thrill from reading of the live burial of 'the stifling of the hundred and twenty-three prisoners in the Black Hole at Calcutta...it is the fact... – it is the *history which excites*' (Poe 1845 [2004], 356, emphasis added). The uncanniness of historical human-on-human violence is delineated in Bettelheim's work *Recollections and Reflections* (1992) in which he reflects on culture through the cruelty and violence humans have shown themselves capable. In the chapter, 'Freedom from Ghetto Thinking' (243–71), he writes that of the importance of:

> ...the feeling of community beyond our own group, beyond iron curtains – not because all men are basically good, but because violence is as natural to man as the tendency toward order. (271).

This violent 'tendency' of humans is what drives preparedness: the preparedness vision is of the other as primarily violent, trans-genocidal and ultimately against the status quo of white supremacy.

Research questions and methodology

Counter-narrative story 2 above, of BME 7/7 experience, demonstrated preparedness in action as delineated in the last paragraph: the need to fly in the face of the fear of what had happened is translated into a potentially criminal act by another; the immediacy of verbal actions against the other in case all raced others are in league against the status quo. That racism increases during an emergency is thus demonstrated, however the research question underlying my ethnographic journal was to question whether ethnic status during an emergency reflects accurately the culture of race underlying the same culture during peace time, whether in fact the *buried alive* metaphor reflects life as it does in counter-narrative story 1 above. The methodology of research required a central focus on race and using the tools of counter-narrative, as offered by CRT. CRT is itself *buried alive* in academia in its reception and treatment, however in this article, and in the ERSC study, CRT conceptions of both policy and society were seen to be crucial in analysis of UK preparedness in terms of race. The tool of counter-narrative was seen as a necessity within preparedness, both as a meaningful way of incorporating the absent other, but also as a methodology of transformation. The necessity of this, regardless of race, was confirmed by the gestures towards meaning in the words and actions of individual players within the exercises observed, as detailed later, pointing towards the possibility of a different kind of futurity within preparedness exercise. CRT acknowledges the use of narratives of marginalised voices in analyzing culture in order to focus on race, as a method of critiquing state structures and organisations. This article therefore makes use of a CRT political framework, besides psychoanalytical theory and psychoanalytical literary parallels, in seeking to explore the metaphor of being *buried alive* to answer the following questions: whether the buried alive experience relates only to the minority experience within civil defence; how structural devices are used to produce the experience of being buried alive; whether this could be combated to produce equality of experience.

The frame of the imagination

Using literary fiction narratives, parallel with CRT counter-narrative, is a useful means of drawing out the structure and psychology revealed within the ESRC ethnography, that is the structure and psychology of racism and also sexism. The violent frame of the literary imagination evoking the inner workings of the human generally is revealed through the tragic performance of characters as shown by Freud in 'Psychopathic Characters on the Stage' (1905–6 [1997b], 87–93). In UK preparedness fictional characters are used within narratives in performative exercises produced to practice how civil defence works in order to strengthen national resilience in the case of a projected emergency. These fictional characters and their reception by staff during the exercises are pivotal to an understanding of the culture of preparedness. Fictional narratives may be analysed on a number of levels, the interest of this article is in how fiction reproduces culture and represents the othered character. In exploring the concept of being *buried alive* in this section I examine how this concept has been evoked in the past in nineteenth century popular fiction, and whether parallels may be drawn with the earlier CRT counter-narratives in this chapter and with contemporary preparedness events; this develops the idea of the psychological concept of the authoritarian patriarchal state apparatus, which then aids the analysis of the research findings later in this article.

In the chapter 'Buried Alive' (Braddon 1862 [2008], 382–94), in the popular Victorian sensation novel *Lady Audley's Secret*, the metaphor *buried alive* is brought to life as the eternal live imprisonment of the other: the Lady Audley of the title. Her incarceration, facilitated by legal means, is seen to be essential to ensure the security of a racially pure, class secure, hetero-normative status quo as underlined by CRT. Her live imprisonment collates all four of my earlier categories of being *buried alive*: the womb-like space, a seeming mistake, the everyday, and the terminal of death.

Sensation novels of the Victorian era dealt with the social and political issues of the role of women at that time, a group of humans subdivided by gender, *buried alive* for their own protection; this is demonstrated in this key chapter of the novel. As Skilton writes the chapter itself is a meta-fictional response to the writer's limits on where to go with this gendered character at that time (2008, xvi). Skilton cites Elaine Showalter's analysis of the centre of the novel, 'Lady Audley's real secret is that she is sane, and, moreover, representative' (xvi), as such she is seen as a threat to society. Here the psychoanalytical literary frame parallels the CRT construction of culture in that the other is seen in 'a socio-literary syndrome' (xvi): to protect the privileged the other must be seen as mad and must be positioned as a character in such a way that others must not be encouraged to identify with them (xvi). This evokes Ahmed's analysis of diversity in the educational workplace and how research knowledge is viewed when it critiques the sphere of academia (2009).

Braddon's key chapter is both metaphor and demonstration of being *buried alive*. The reader is taken on a journey with the main protagonist into her prison of being *buried alive* in another country, rather like the prisoners of the USA held in Guantanamo Bay were seen as outside of the Geneva conventions on the coast of Cuba. The reader experiences the journey from the inside of the experience, just as the chapter's title is buried inside the book named after her secret.

> 'Where are you going to take me?' she asked, at last. 'I am tired of being treated like some naughty child, who is put into a dark cellar as a punishment for its offences. Where are you taking me?'
>
> 'To a place in which you will have ample leisure to repent the past...'
> (Braddon 1862 [2008], 385)

Lady Audley knows what's happening to her and the metaphor she uses to describe how she feels is prophetic of her incarceration, and the intended effect on her mind of a human experience that must be a mistake, but is the everyday of the other: "'I know where you have brought me ... This is a

MAD-HOUSE.'" (387). The description of where she is to brought to stay is curiously womb-like in some ways, but it is a womb where a child is destined to die, the premature burial of life as still-born. The adjectives and phrases, 'black and white marble,' 'funereal,' 'gloomy,' and a 'bed so wondrously made, as to appear to have no opening...unless the counterpane had been slit asunder with a penknife' (388–9), evoke a reverse birth, a Caesarean of death; the returning of someone from whence they came, so reminiscent of the repatriation policies of far right groups in Europe and the USA.

Lady Audley's response to this place of incarceration is to become 'sullen and angry' (389) as her name is taken away from her (389–90) like the slaves of the Western colonies as seen in the colonial gaze; even her use of French is seen 'better fitted to her mood and to herself than...English' (391). She accuses Robert of him having *buried* her *alive*, that he '"used...power basely and cruelly, and have brought me to a living grave"' (391): the terminal of death. Robert explains why he has imprisoned her this way, because he cannot be 'a traitor to society' (391) and leave her free, epitomising how the 'race traitor' analysis of CRT (Bell 1992, 114) is reflexive. Lady Audley ends by saying 'that law could pronounce no worse sentence than this, a life-long imprisonment in a mad-house' (Braddon 1862 [2008], 394). The metaphor *buried alive* displays both the act of supremacy in its production via the physical restriction of others, but also the act of imagining of racism and sexism, the supremacist construction of the other; the metaphor thus performs how imagined fear is projected on to the screen of life: the gendered or raced incarceration of those who threaten the social order becomes a necessity. Bell, in his '*Epilogue: Beyond Despair,*' cites 'Huggins (who) argues that Americans view history as linear and evolutionary and tend to see slavery and racism as an aberration or pathological condition' (1992, 196, my parenthetical addition). Both cultures of the imagination and of the lived experience demonstrate that in many ways life is not evolving progressively for all, and that acts of violence against targeted cultural groups are not isolated but emerge from human group psychology. Bell writes of the idea of '*both, and,*' that is the necessity to acknowledge the 'futility of action' with the necessity 'that action must be taken' (1992, 199) to combat inequality and racism. This epitomises the metaphor of *buried alive*: to overcome the experience of this concept we have to acknowledge and state the place we're in – inequality, how it is constructed and by whom, beside this we have to acknowledge the place we want to get to, to look beyond inequality, towards an imagined state of equality. To accomplish this it is essential to deconstruct the outer reaches of inequality, and these are enshrined in national preparedness.

The study

As I have detailed in other work the vast majority of personnel observed within the ethnography were white, and therefore in many ways what is critiqued is about whiteness (Chakrabarty 2010, 5), however, the existence of 'race' appeared briefly in images used on Powerpoints during fictional exercises and as characters within those scenarios; 'race' also cropped up in cultural references made by participants during the study, and this included indirect self-referential comments within reflection on the process of preparedness. The ethnography turned then to analyse these fragments of race and to explore what this almost absence of race means for cultures of preparedness, but above all I (noting that I take the passive voice out of this decision and acknowledge that there are multiple interpretations of what is to come in this article) look at what or who is *buried alive* in preparedness. These fragments of race are analysed to expose their role and function in the narratives of raced bodies within preparedness. The research questions corporate, governmental and individual assumptions underlying UK preparedness. Questions are asked of the nature of whiteness within the roles played, the function of whiteness within the scenarios played out in preparation for emergency, and the narratives of whiteness within civil defence pedagogies. This article now goes on to look at the explicit meanings of the key themes of civil defence preparedness when confronted with an absence of raced personnel within a wall of whiteness – what constitutes emergency, the necessity of preparation, and the type of state that needs defence – and explores what this means for the futurity of race and minority cultures who are *buried alive*.

Research findings

1. A character buried alive in the safe womb of a tabletop exercise, in the terminal of death

Preparedness is an area of education which epitomises the way a state sees its citizens, and which citizens it views as outside of the state. In the ESRC study what was interesting was that race is hardly mentioned, thus when race is mentioned it is crucial to the analysis of the policy. In all the exercises attended BME participants were scarce if nonexistent and, if present, none played important roles in the exercises such as organisers or major professional participants. For example in the Department of Health *'Exercise Peak Practice'* (2009a) the only mention of race was indirect, one character in the media text for the fictional scenario that the participants worked through on the exercise. At this particular point during the scenario two children die of swine flu two days after being turned away from a hospital and being refused treatment. One is a white girl, Holly, and the other is a seven-year-old Asian boy, 'Jaye Patel.' Holly's father is shown to be angry about the treatment of his daughter, he says, 'we followed the guidelines,' but the Asian child is seen without parents or community apart from the school head teacher, who says that Jaye 'was new to the area' and that the children 'will not be forgotten.' Jaye is seen only as a victim of the illness, not in relation to the wider world of families and communities. His being 'new to the area' was never unpicked; was he imagined as a refugee, or had his family just moved home? In reality the other pertinent aspects of this particular exercise would impact on race too: for example, the time before burial/cremation is important in many cultures and religions, and in the event of a swine flu epidemic there would be the potential for a backlog of bodies in mortuaries. Besides the latter issue Asian parents are as likely to react as white parents. In this case what was interesting was that race was dead when it entered the exercise – a corpse without relatives as mourners, a corpse whose race is washed away in death like blood on a mortuary floor; 'Jaye' is an automaton of race, an uncanny reverse of the white child, who is imagined as mourned by family and community. 'Jaye' is *buried alive*, a still posthumous absence of race; he is used as a statistic, not a breathing presence, he and his kin are buried under the experience of the kin of 'Holly': even in the multicultural fiction of preparedness humans are imagined as different and unequal.

2. Professionals' experience buried alive within preparedness, the everyday of being a professional

A major aspect of multicultural society, besides cultures of race and class, is the diversity of different cultures or social groupings. One participant interviewed in the ESRC study, 'Professional 2,' made the point that preparedness public education, like the government publications and media campaigns, such as *Important Information about Swine Flu* (Department of Health 2009b), have not taken account of these multi-cultures of groupings in metropolitan cities, in particular foreign students, refugees, people without families, and gay people perhaps estranged from their families. There is an assumption that people have contact with particular community leaders such as via places of worship, or they live with others, whereas the reality is that that is an assumption of the cold war era: 'How you get that kind of community resilience going in a geographical region that doesn't have a defined community has been unanswered' ('Professional 2' 2009). There is also an assumption that not only do we each have defined communities (e.g. you look like you're a Muslim therefore you can get help from a mosque) but also that the community will welcome you with open arms (e.g. what if you are gay and Muslim, or gay and black, will your local mosque or church welcome you with open arms when you need help during a flu pandemic?)

The issue of who is being prepared for emergency is crucial to the analysis of UK preparedness as this pinpoints racial destiny and evidence of equitable futurity; the evidence points towards a simplistic and superficial understanding of diversity that would impact negatively in the case of emergency. The swine flu example is a pertinent one here as the policy assumed that individuals were part of a wider community who would pick up medication and food for those who were confined by the illness (Department of Health 2009b) and surgeries were telling those infected to stay away; those infected but disconnected from mainstream community groups were therefore *buried alive* at home with a potentially fatal illness.

3. About cultural wish fulfilment, and of destiny in cultures of diversity: it's not a mistake, it's your own fault

At this point it is worth referring to what is perceived, in terms of equality of destiny, in the words of those who we would hope might have a positive view of equality. In the period I was working on the ESRC study many BME people were listening carefully to the words of politicians' speeches, particularly those of the first non-white President of the USA, however, his philosophy was epitomised in the phrase 'Your destiny is in your hands' in 2009 (The White House 2009, 3). President Obama, in the midst of speaking about governmental actions towards equality and how expectations are unequal, said:

> If you live in a poor neighbourhood, you will face challenges that somebody in a wealthy suburb does not have to face. But...no one has written your destiny for you. Your destiny is in your hands.
> (The White House 2009, 3)

Obama's message echoed the words of Michelle Obama, earlier in the year, to a hall of schoolgirls, during the G20 in London: 'By getting a good education, you too can control your own destiny' (Elizabeth Garrett Anderson Language College 2009). Michelle Obama's uncanny message is however underlined by being embodied in her name, *buried alive* within the name of her husband; the meaning of her live speech, dies prematurely, when we read his name on her body, her marital status stages a denial of equal futurity; just as her words and his words, although acknowledging inequality, show the hopes of raced bodies to be *buried alive* in their skins.

Preparedness materials are based on the exclusion via destiny of many via the construction of a fictional reality of sameness as evoked by diversity image making. In the case of civil defence this is dangerous as those excluded from the preparedness scenario in the performative rehearsal of exercise are those ultimately excluded and annihilated in the reality of lived experience as Hurricane Katrina in 2005 demonstrated (Marable 2008).

4. Professionals, equality and the survival of white supremacy: the preparedness bunker as terminal of death

Leaders in preparedness education are seen in this study to reject criticism of the explicit assumptions underlying their work; the organisation and construction of the exercises also reflect a level of continuity since the cold war. This was surprising for me as my experience of education is that educationalists tend to see educational work as a work in progress, and educational research documents the adaptation process to the changing needs of the present, and towards a perceived futurity, even if that futurity is seen to be thwarted in some way through raced experience as shown through CRT (Gillborn 2008). In preparedness, as 'Professional 2' said, often exercises:

> ...are very rarely genuine training exercises, and so there's a real resistance to any criticism being made. The people on there aren't prepared to be criticised and don't want any of their vulnerabilities exposed. And that's the problem with training and exercises in general.
>
> ('Professional 2' 2009)

Some of the preparedness professionals viewed their work within a wider sphere of training and exercises that might be run by other professionals; they acknowledged that educational processes progress through revealing what is obscured by surface rhetoric, and through intervention by outsider views. Sometimes the preparedness professionals saw themselves as privileged outsiders, drawn into preparedness exercise through their expertise, but destined for terminal exclusion, to be ultimately *buried alive*. These individuals were indirectly empathetic with the minority experience within the majority experience, and also viewed themselves as part of the vast majority whose destiny, in the event of extreme emergency, would be death, unlike those whose survival is prepared for in the nuclear bunker.

'Professional 1' had been involved in scientific research in preparedness during the cold war. He talked to me about the development of nuclear bunkers and about their development in an exercise in the Nevada desert. He was very clear with me about how difficult it was to produce bunkers that would withstand the kind of nuclear devices being developed, and thus our conversation became more philosophical about survival and the meaning of preparing to survive in a nuclear age. As I was a teenager during the era of the documents he had worked on I was also aware of the culture at the time in which he was working, indeed at school we had been alerted to the very document he talked about. So I asked him whether as a government scientist he would have been given a place in the bunker in the event of a nuclear war whilst working on *Protect and Survive* (Central Office of Information 1975). He said no, then he paused. When he spoke again it was to answer that he would not want to be in the bunker anyway, he'd want to get home, to be with his family. As he said this I felt what was implicit was that he wouldn't want to be *buried alive*, he knows who's going to be there and he doesn't particularly want to die with them. As a scientist, he knew how the science of bombs so quickly outstrips the science and engineering of any shelters. He could see inside the structures of civil defence, and didn't want to be there, the idea of death was strangely better than living amongst white supremacists.

It is what is left unsaid often that uncannily clarifies the ethos underlying civil defence education: that to survive a nuclear war, if at all possible, given the development of more powerful nuclear bombs than were used on Nagasaki, would mean living in a bunker with other government officials and creating a new world without our chosen families. It is an extreme preparedness of eugenics, the careful selection of survival of the most powerful, and this preparedness prepares for the annihilation of those who threaten that survival, shown here in an interview concerning preparedness work on *Protect and Survive* (Central Office of Information 1975):

> I mean, there's a lot of tales told...that commissioners in headquarters had the right to shoot people if they come.... Rowdy crowds and all this sort of thing. And they would have the authority to put down riots if they thought best.... That always had implications that the police and the army would go out and do the business. ('Professional 2' 2009)

What the latter interview made explicit is that civil defence leadership involves deciding who has the right to survive, and preparing strategies against those who might assert their right to equal resources after a disaster. *Buried alive* in preparedness documents is a hierarchical survival plan, this plan is the inverse of any diversity document. The real resilience agenda if it was graphically produced would resemble the current raced and gendered hierarchy of privilege in the UK; if you took this chart and sliced off the line at the top you could imagine the occupants of the nuclear bunker. Most of this pyramid shape, everyone below the top line, would be buried alive (no italics this time) like the Iraqis within the Wikileaks 'Warlogs' (2010), apart from a few service personnel, who would no doubt provide the apocalyptic breeding ground for racial survival.

5. Survival myths and the burial of diversity

Some of the professionals in the ESRC study seemed to see preparedness as partly about upholding the myth of diversity, just like the myth of survival in a nuclear age. I saw this as parallel within the context of education, where myths are also propagated that despite unequal educational experience, such as class sizes and resources, success is based mainly on individual effort as epitomised in the Obamas' speeches in 2009. In preparedness the major myth that is promoted is that of majority survival. For example in 'Preparedness Exercise 3' at a major UK airport in October 2009, something seemed unbelievable about the character actions within the scenario: as I observed from the sidelines in the darkness technicians simulated a plane exploding, quite soon afterwards a group of people were led away to safety. I queried the outcome as I stood with a group of observers coughing in the smoke from the flames still emerging from the burning plane carcass. A fire specialist from another airport said that if a plane really exploded just after take off – the scenario at this exercise – there would be very few survivors, if any, as the tank would be full of fuel, however the exercise and therefore the training for staff, was based on many survivors. Like a piece of absurd drama the exercise transformed for me at this point into a strange game, a war game where we were all engaged in watching something that would never happen, like a disaster movie in which we were extras; the perform-ativity of the exercise confirmed the link with the entertainment industry is a valid one, just as Hollywood disaster movies are designed to make us feel good as someone who we identify with survives, preparedness drugs us up in a similar way so that we don't ask difficult questions about our individual futurity.

The preparedness survival myth is particularly highlighted where diversity is concerned. Race was absent from the latter airport scenario, all survivors were treated equally it appeared within the exercise, even though when disas-ters occur, race – since 9/11 and 7/7 in particular – is a major differential as victims may also be seen by preparedness professionals as potential guilty parties. The other aspect of this difference is in the gaze of the Western media reporting on race, echoing the culture of the contemporary moment. During the events following the Asian tsunami of December 2004 there were differences in particular over the treatment of tourists versus the indigenous populations of the affected countries as Peter Wilby examined in *The Guard-ian* (2005). Wilby pointed out that 'It takes a tsunami to interest Europeans in loss of life in Asia. That does not mean…that we value white lives more than black or brown lives – at least not in a racist way,' going on to state that the media sees British citizens as having 'the same world outlook as the overwhelmingly white Anglo-Saxon people it employs' (Wilby 2005) even though, as Wilby acknowledges, the UK population is diverse and therefore individuals may feel more identification with non-British others.

During 'Preparedness Exercise 3' the only (indirect) mention of race was when one of the participant organisers explained that language help lines would be set up to deal with survivor and relative language issues in this incident. He then went on to explain why they had decided to attach specific workers to each survivor; he gave the example of the survivors returning from the tsunami in 2004, many of whom returned with no passports, keys to homes, or indeed any form of identification, and having lost their entire nuclear families – it was felt important to have a single point of contact for these people as they were inevitably in a vulnerable state. The airport worker was obviously very moved by his experience of working at the airport during the aftermath of the tsunami and had a humanitarian response. However, this personal response to the tsunami, translated into the scenario of 'Prepared-ness Exercise 3,' seemed impossible in terms of the authorities' response in the current climate; an event like the explosion of a plane departing a major UK airport would, after 9/11, provoke a race alert and as such any BME sur-vivors and their relatives could be seen as suspects to the atrocity, rather than victims; guilty until proved innocent. We know that by the evening the 7 July 2005 suicide bombings on the London transport system police quickly started to label it a suicidal terror attack as they made deductions from the phone calls of Asian parents from the north of the UK, worried that their sons had not returned after day trips to London. Subsequent media reports have revealed a clichéd response to these British Asian parents: rather than treating them as grieving families who knew nothing about the plans of their adult offspring they are seen as guilty by association. Their situation is a parallel to the underachieving students of an unequal education system who are seen as responsible for their situation through their lack of effort as noted in the Obamas' 2009 speeches. *Buried alive* in this is that race dictates destiny in an emergency, but also in other times too.

Conclusion – resilient resistance to being *buried alive*

A cultural agenda towards futurity involves professionals, both those involved in education and those involved in preparedness, to take on board the absence of race and start the work of translating its presence towards a futurity of real equality of opportunity. This will involve looking at representation in personnel, the absence of BME staff in pedagogical practice and the relation between visual raced presence and the curriculum. Physical representation has to go in tandem however with myth deconstruction: the word equality has to mean equality. In preparedness cultures in a nuclear age this is impossible, weapons mean power, but they also mean the termination at some point of the entire human race. However, as this article has demonstrated, the psychoanalysis of preparedness may be translated into other spheres, like education, where the same issues, of racial resilience, myth deconstruction, personnel, and futurity, apply. Like preparedness cultures, education has at its heart futurity, and a futurity of equality would not bury some alive for the survival of the few; an educational futurity of equality would involve equal education for all, involving the abolition of private education, producing equal access to university despite race and class. Like the undressing of the myths of civil defence education, a futurity of equal survival would involve exploding pseudo-scientific myths on race and intelligence, the *buried alive* of racism.

Just as the state practices the unimaginable as a means to combat potential threats to survival through preparedness, CRT educationalists too could learn from this process by exploring the extremities of the burial of race, as the sensation novelists of the Victorian era explored the burial of the other and its resurgence in crime. Through educational research it is possible to predict the imaginable in terms of education, that is the present system of unequal education continuing has predictable outcomes in terms of equality of life opportunity based on race, class and gender. In contrast a fictional future scenario in the USA and UK would be an equal education system, where the economically well off and those who are living on welfare, would all get a guarantee that their children would get an equal education, and that destiny would no longer be shaped by birth, but by the individual endeavour promoted by the Obamas' speeches of 2009.

Education and preparedness are the extreme binaries of cultural policy: the one projecting into the future, the other imagining end-of-the-world scenarios. Racial absence within cultural policy is uncanny: by assuming that citizens are all the same, but are really treated differently, policy withdraws citizenship from many and simultaneously produces the frustrated and ultimately aggressive other of which the authoritarian has most fear, as shown by the events of 2001: the metaphor was reversed back on to the Western citizens *buried alive* during the attacks on the World Trade Centre on 9/11. This article puts forward the case for future preparedness/education to take into account the new era of equality since the dawning of the age of Obama; removing fear of the raced other from emergency preparedness/education would produce a different culture and a more assured futurity for all.

Notes

1. The names of the professionals and others interviewed or observed in the ESRC study, and reported on in this article, are masked by the technical term 'Professional' or 'Participant,' and numbered; this is due to the confidential nature of their work. Generally academic writers rename participants in their work, however my personal feeling about this is that rather than renaming real people with bland names I would rather highlight the fact that I am extracting their words and using them in another context; by numbering participants the meta-fictional aspects of academic writing are brought to the fore. The real person behind the study is thus *buried alive*; and the theme of this article is recreated, *mise en abyme*.
2. A number of terms are used to describe this work: preparedness, civil defence, disaster education, and resilience.
3. Names and places have been changed to preserve the confidentiality of participants in both the CRT counter-narratives; I reversed my general feelings about this issue of naming participants when I came to what appear to be stories. It is as if, like inside the womb or the nuclear bunker of a text, a character can be named and is safe within the confines of what appears to have a beginning, middle and an end.
4. This was known only afterwards; at the time there were reports of power failures being behind the initial events.

References

Ahmed, S. 2009. Embodying diversity: Problems and paradoxes for black feminists. *Race Ethnicity and Education* 12, no. 1: 41–52.

Bell, D.A. 1992. *Faces at the bottom of the well: The permanence of racism*. New York: Basic Books.

Bettelheim, B. 1992. *Recollections and reflections*. London: Penguin.

Braddon, M.E. 2008 [1862]. *Lady Audley's secret*. Oxford: Oxford World Classics.

Central Office of Information. 1975. *Protect and survive*. http://www.screenonline.org.uk/film/id/724975/index.html.

Chakrabarty, N. 2010. Theatre of survival: Preparedness participation and white supremacy. Paper presented at NYU Forum on Citizenship and Applied Theatre, April 25, in Steinhardt School, New York University, New York.

Department of Health. 2009a. Exercise peak practice. http://www.dh.gov.uk/en/Publication-sandstatistics/Publications/ PublicationsPolicyAndGuidance/DH_108948.

Department of Health. 2009b. Important information about Swine Flu. http://www.nhs.uk/news/2009/4april/documentsswine%20flu%20leaflet_web%20version.pdf.

Elizabeth Garrett Anderson Language College. 2009. *Michelle Obama – Michelle Obama Visit*. [Video]. http://www.egaschool.co.uk/page.php?2.

Freud, S. 1997a [1919]. The uncanny. In *Writings on art and literature*. Trans. and ed. J. Strachey, 193–233. Stanford, CA: Stanford University Press.

Freud, S. 1997b [1905–6]. Psychopathic characters on the stage. In *Writings on art and literature*. Trans. and ed. J Strachey, 87–93. Stanford, CA: Stanford University Press.

Gillborn, D. 2008. *Racism and education: Coincidence or conspiracy?* Abingdon: Routledge.

Marable, M. 2008. Introduction: Seeking higher ground: Race, public policy and the Hurricane Katrina crisis. In *Seeking higher ground: The Hurricane Katrina crisis, race and public policy reader*, ed. M. Marable and K. Clarke, ix–xvi. Basingstoke: Palgrave.

Poe, E.A. 2004. The premature burial. In *The selected writings of Edgar Allan Poe*, ed. G.R. Thompson, 356–67. London: W.W. Norton.

Preston, J., B. Avery, N. Chakrabarty, and C. Edmonds. 2010. Preparedness as public pedagogy. Paper presented at The British Educational Research Association Conference, September 1–4, at the University of Warwick.

Royle, N. 2003. Buried alive. In *The uncanny*, N. Royle, 142–71. Manchester: Manchester University Press.

Skilton, D. 2008. Introduction. In *Lady Audley's secret*, M.E. Braddon, vii–xxiii. Oxford: Oxford World Classics.

Wikileaks. 2010. MURDER OF%%% by -%%% in ():%%% CIV KILLED, %%%CF INJ/DAM, in *Warlogs*. http://warlogs.wikileaks.org/id/498E68F2-DA34-421C-ABA [7#sq0F8B93514FB7/.

Wilby, P. 2005. Foreign news a distant memory. *The Guardian*, July 25. http://www.guardian.co.uk/media/2005/jul/25/mondaymediasection7.

The White House. 2009, 17 July. Remarks by the President to the NAACP Centennial Convention. [Transcript]. http://www.whitehouse.gov.

Zizek, S. 2002. *Welcome to the desert of the real*. London: Verso.

The invisibility of race: intersectional reflections on the liminal space of alterity

Nicola Rollock

It has been argued that racialised Others occupy a liminal space of alterity; a position at the edges of society from which their identities and experiences are constructed. Rather than being regarded as a place of disadvantage and degradation, it has been posited that those excluded from the centre can experience a 'perspective advantage' as their experiences and analyses become informed by a panoramic dialectic offering a wider lens than the white majority located in the privileged spaces of the centre are able to deploy. In this article, I invite the reader to glimpse the world from this liminal positioning as I reflect critically on how the intersections between social class, race and gender variously advantage or disadvantage, depending on the context, the ways in which Black middle classes are able to engage with the education system. While I make reference to findings from a recent school-focused ESRC project 'The Educational Strategies of the Black Middle Classes'[1] the article takes a wider perspective of the education system, also incorporating an autobiographical analysis of the academy as a site of tension, negotiation and challenge for the few Black middle classes therein. I make use of the Critical Race Theory tool of chronicling (counter-narrative) to help demonstrate the complex, multifaceted and often contradictory ways in which ambitions for race equality often represent lofty organisational ideals within which genuine understanding of racism is lacking.

I am invisible, understand, simply because people refuse to see me. (...) When they approach me they see only my surroundings, themselves, or figments of their imagination – indeed, everything and anything except me. (...) Nor is my invisibility exactly a matter of bio-chemical accident to my epidermis. That invisibility to which I refer occurs because of a peculiar disposition of the eyes of those with whom I come in contact. A matter of the construction of their inner eyes, those eyes with which they look through their physical eyes upon reality. (...) It is sometimes advantageous to be unseen, although it is most often rather wearing on the nerves. Then too, you're constantly being bumped against by those of poor vision (...) You ache with the need to convince yourself that you do exist in the real world, that you're a part of all the sound and anguish, and you strike out with your fists, you curse and you swear to make them recognize you. And, alas, it's seldom successful.

Ralph Ellison (1965, 7)

Introduction

Drawing on Wynter's (1992) theorisation of the concept of marginality, Ladson-Billings and Donnor 2008, 373) posit that racialised others occupy a 'liminal space of alterity' that is, a position at the edges of society from which their identities and experiences are constructed. They remain at the margins through acts and frequent reminders from dominant groups that regardless of achievement, qualification or status they are locked in 'the power dynamic and hierarchical racial structures' that serve to maintain unequal order in society (Ladson-Billings and Donnor 2008, 372).

Yet Wynter (1992) insists that rather than regarding this space as a site of dismal subjugation, those excluded from the centre can experience a certain profound analytical insight that is 'beyond the normative boundary of the conception of Self/Other' (Ladson-Billings and Donnor 2008, 373). In other words, it is precisely from this position in the margins that racialised others are able to acquire not simply an 'oppositional world-view' (hooks 1990, 149) but what might be understood as a unique *surround vision* that is able to recognise and deconstruct the multifaceted contours of Whiteness and therefore advance the broader objectives of the racial justice project. Such an all-encompassing analytic perspective is particularly important to challenge and move beyond the *not seeing* nature of Whiteness that works to perpetuate a racially inequitable status quo:

> One of the most powerful and dangerous aspects of whiteness is that many (possibly the majority) of white people have no awareness of whiteness as a construction, let alone their own role in sustaining and playing out the inequities at the heart of whiteness. (Gillborn 2005, 9)

While recognising and fully supporting the centrality of liminality to advancing a 'counter-hegemonic discourse' (hooks 1990, 149), I seek in this article to provide an extension to these debates by arguing that the very notion of what might be framed as *liminality as resistance* is wholly context dependent. That is to say, the field in which racialised others are operating, the tools or resources at their disposal, the support mechanisms available to them and the relative power of other actors present within the social space or field fundamentally impacts and brings into awkward tension the extent to which occupying a site in the margins becomes advantageous. I variously employ Bourdieu and Critical Race Theory (CRT) as theoretical frames of reference. As such, the arguments presented are located in an understanding, informed by CRT, that racism operates as normal[2] in everyday life (Delgado and Stefancic 2001; Tate IV 1997) and can, in part, be understood through the various forms of capital – to borrow from Bourdieu – that are positioned as having status and legitimacy within formally sanctioned spaces of, for the purposes of this article, the education system which I am taking in its broadest sense to include the academy:

> The members of groups based on co-option (. . .) always have something else in common beyond the characteristics explicitly demanded. The common image of the professions, which is no doubt one of the real determinants of 'vocations,' is less abstract and unreal than that presented by statisticians; it takes into account not only the nature of the job and the income, but *those secondary characteristics which are often the basis of their social value (. . .) and which, though absent from the official job description, function as tacit requirements, such as age, sex, social or ethnic origin. . .* (Bourdieu 1984, 102; emphasis added)

As a theory, CRT affords me, as a scholar of colour, the license and power to 'speak back' about racial inequalities in a way that hitherto I have not found entirely possible through many other theoretical tools. Critical Race Theory offers a framework that explicitly recognises and encourages people of colour to name, speak and theorise about their experiences as shaped by racism. The approach I adopt, therefore, is creative what Tate IV (1997, 210) describes as an 'enactment of hybridity.' I use part autobiography, part data analysis and part counter-narrative to critically interrogate the norms and practices of educational spaces of which I have been part, am part and, predominantly due to my racially minoritised status, am not part. As a Black female academic, I am at once located within this article even as I write hence the use, where appropriate, of pronouns such 'we,' 'our,' 'my.' With reference to data analysis, I draw on findings from a two-year ESRC project 'The Educational Strategies of the Black Middle Classes' which examines the educational perspectives, strategies and experiences of Black Caribbean heritage middle class families as they attempt to navigate their children successfully through the school system. Many of the parents' accounts speak directly to the notion of marginality and how they have developed a complex set of resources with which to manage instances of racism and othering. By drawing these strands of analysis together I am seeking to highlight the pervasiveness of the racial power dynamics at play across the education system as a whole.

There is an additional point to be made. In seeking to capture some of the multifaceted, nuanced and quite complex ways which facilitate the continued existence of race inequality and demonstrate how racialised others manage such experiences, this article attempts an ambitious project. It is near impossible to present such complexity in precise conventional terms with a neat beginning, revolutionary middle and an all-encompassing conclusion; the racial justice project is challenging and it is ongoing hence the naming of this article as a set of 'reflections.' There is no tidy conclusion.

Finally, I invite the reader to consider this article an enterprise in seeking to critically 'name, reflect on and dismantle discourses of Whiteness' (Leonardo 2002, 31) and to not only consider what is written here in a mere academic way but to take account of how their own racial positioning (and awareness thereof) informs how they make sense of and react to the arguments presented.

Understanding liminality

In an attempt to deconstruct and give life to some of the theoretical analyses with which I began this article, I begin with a true story and reflect on the notion of marginality as it came to pertain to my own raced and classed positioning and also how aspects of my gender came to have salience to my identity.

Part I – the true story

When I was precisely eight and a half years old my parents moved me from my local state primary school – a place where, in my nostalgic memory, we played kiss chase at break time, lay on our backs in the field daydreaming at the sky in the summer and where all the kids lived in roughly the same size houses and our dads drove the same kinds of cars – and sent me instead to a private girls' school that seemed, to my young mind, to be an eternity away. The only Black teacher at the state school had warned my parents about the pervasiveness of racism, of how it was affecting her and many Black pupils she knew. I had no idea what racism was but I do remember that my (white) teacher refused to allow me to move up to the next set of *Peter and Jane* books because I was racing ahead of the rest of the class. 'Read them again,' I was instructed. When I told my parents my mum looked at my dad but said nothing.

So to my new school. I arrived on a Monday morning. Monday was spelling day; a test of 20 words that had been given to the girls as weekend homework on the Friday. To the utter amazement of the girl with whom I had swapped to mark our work, I got all 20 correct and won myself a shiny gold star next to my name on the chart on the wall behind Mrs Jackson's desk. I also won the instant friendship of Lucy Gladstone-Brown,[3] Ms Popularity herself. I would recall later how on our way home on the bus one day Lucy pointed out her home. It was massive three-storey sand-coloured affair, standing far enough back from the road to allow two or three generous sized cars to lounge comfortably on the drive. 'Wow,' I said peering through the bus window, 'It's huge!' 'Well, we can't live in a bungalow,' Lucy retorted, her voice frosted with a disgust, that I hadn't known possible in an eight-year-old, at the mere thought. I recalled feeling a bit odd about what she had said. Why hadn't she just agreed that it was a big house? Why had she uttered the words with such condescension? It occurred to me that maybe Lucy shouldn't see where I lived.

In that first week I settled down with my new best friend and enjoyed school with the rest of the girls. On the Thursday, after break or lunch, I forget which, we sat in our classroom at the top of the rambling old Victorian building in which the school was situated, messing around, giggling and chatting until our teacher Mrs Jackson arrived to take the afternoon register. Whoever I was messing around with tickled me and being horrendously ticklish I let out a shriek accompanied by tumbling notes of carefree laughter. It was at that precise moment that Mrs Jackson walked through the door. Even now I remember the sound of her high heels on the tiled lino. 'Who...?' she boomed in a tones swelled with harshness, '... screamed?' Hush fell upon the class, all earlier tomfoolery and laugher dying without trace, without fulfilment into the now stilled air. We froze, alert to the possibility of something awful that had yet to occur. I swallowed. I would say that someone had tickled me. She would understand. After all, she'd seemed nice enough on Monday when she was awarding me my star. No, I couldn't do that. She would want to know who had tickled me and I wasn't a grass. 'Well?' she boomed. We sat meekly peering up at her wanting to appear attentive yet striving to avoid her inquisitional gaze. Silence. 'It was me,' I finally offered in a small fragile voice, thinking that perhaps I might receive some reprieve being the new girl. She glared at me, 'Well, I don't know where *you* come from but *we* certainly don't do that sort of thing here!' she barked and clonked in her high heels to her desk.

In making this powerful statement, which I will continue shortly to discuss through the eyes of my eight-year-old self, the teacher is in a very Bourdieuian sense letting me know that my act has no place within the 'legitimate culture' of the school:

> ...the educational institution succeeds in imposing cultural practices that it does not teach and does not even explicitly demand, but which belong to the attributes attached by status to the position it assigns, the qualifications it awards and the social positions to which the latter give access. (Bourdieu 1984, 26)

There is a further complex playing out of power here as I unwittingly become positioned as having contributed to my own exclusion by not adhering to the rules, albeit unwritten and unnamed, of the school. Mrs Jackson lets me know that I can – *potentially* – gain 'inclusion,' however, I definitely am not yet on the inside.

The shiny gloss of my newness was ripped from my being as I struggled to make sense of the reprimand. 'Where I come from?' I puzzled and puzzled over this phrase. 'I came from...well I live in Tooting, just near the common, very pretty,' I considered. Why would people in Tooting be more likely to scream than…? No, that didn't make sense. 'We?' Which we? Who were 'we'? Wasn't I 'we' since I was sat in the same classroom, wearing the same khaki green uniform as everyone else? I felt myself shrink behind a veil of confusion, of hurt. I vowed not to speak for the rest of the afternoon and proceeded to study Mrs Jackson carefully, watching her every move, listening to her language, making note of with whom she smiled, taking note of with whom she did not. I studied the rest of the girls in my class, watched how they interacted with Mrs Jackson, with each other. I was determined to make sense of this 'we' of which I apparently was not part. And it was through my observations that I learnt to see this 'we.' I saw how the class was made up mainly of white girls (living in big houses like Lucy's) who had 'Pops Club' pencil cases that you could only buy from a single shop in Wandsworth Common,[4] somewhere I had never ventured; they had scented erasers and Caron d'Ache[5] pencils, which were terribly expensive. My stationery came from Woolworths. I heard how they 'popped over' to their holiday homes in the south of France during half term. I went (with much excitement because I loved books) to Tooting library loosing myself in fictional tales while gorging on penny sweets from the local newsagent. I watched as their 'mummies' came to collect them in green wellies, Burberry jackets or body-warmers making promises of afternoon tea to other mummies. And they were accompanied by small rosy-cheeked boys wearing blond bowl-shaped tussled hair and the blazers of prep[6] schools of which I had (then) never heard. And golden Labradors wagged excited tails in the back of Land Rovers and cars whose identities I could not place.

I begin to hate my dad's car.

This was the 'we' of which I was not part.

I tell this story, occurring as it does over 30 years ago, as a reflection of how I came to class awareness and the beginnings of my understanding of the power and taken-for-granted privileges embedded in Whiteness. As has been argued at length elsewhere (McIntosh 1997; Wildman and Davis 1997; Leonardo 2002), Whiteness tends to benefit and advantage whites in ways that they seldom see or care to acknowledge. However, my schooling enabled me to not only see Whiteness but understand and develop a level of perception and analyses of how middle class whites engage with one another, the language they use, the pastimes and activities they pursue, their tastes and preferences (Bourdieu 1984) and, significantly, how they treated people who were not like them. It was only much later, despite incessant warnings from the handful of Black girls advising me of which teachers I should remain vigilant and hearing various accounts of racist incidents, that I began to explicitly recognise myself as racialised and, consequently, comprehend how race and class came together in quite complex ways with varying and uneven outcomes depending on your racialised status.

Transferring from a co-educational state school to an independent girls' school enabled me to forge a comprehension of intersectionality[7] and acts of class distinction, shaped as they are by race, long before I learnt and deployed, with some discomfort and resistance, the formally 'sanctioned' theoretical language of the academy without which my racialised experiences apparently had little legitimacy. The African American scholar bell hooks speaks to similar discomforts when she observes 'this language that enabled me to attend graduate school, to write a dissertation, to speak at job interviews, carries the scent of oppression' (hooks 1990, 146).

However, there was a further aspect of my identity to which, at the time, I paid scant attention; that of femininity. Attending an independent girls' school meant I became embedded in discourses of femininity that were predominantly white and middle class. I was teased to the point of anxious self-consciousness about the shape and size of my bottom; my skirt not so much as A-line as awkward pencil-cut thanks to my derriere. Hair was also a subject of white curiosity. How often did I wash it? How long did it take to style and in moments that struck an as yet unanalysed peril in my heart, could they touch it? While white girls flicked their hair or dried it in seconds under the dryer when we went swimming, I and the other Black girls attempted to restore ours to some natural order before, the job yet incomplete, being barked back into hurried lines by impatient gym teachers. These experiences, regardless of school type, location or gender intake, mirror those recounted during interviews with many of the Black middle class parents in the project 'The Educational Strategies of the Black Middle Classes':

> I remember children coming up to me to find out if my bottom was white or Black because they just had no idea at all (...) I always remember that (...) I couldn't believe that anyone could be so ignorant as to not know (...) they were shocked about my hair not being the same as theirs. (...) they were just intrigued about me as a person and in turn I was intrigued that they didn't know... (Vanessa, Community Development Officer)

Like the parents in the project, these daily moments of othering were not limited to the relatively unmonitored spaces of the playground but were also evident within the classroom. I remember how the musical tastes (classical) of the parents' of a handful of über-trendy, pretty, blond-haired, clique-y girls served to imbue them with a set of unspoken 'secondary characteristics' (Bourdieu 1984, 102) that amounted to boundless status and privilege in our music lessons; they were seldom told off and given countless opportunities to talk ad infinitem about music and skiing holidays while the rest of us sat restlessly in the dull greyness of the shadows. My parents clearly did not have the 'right' taste in music for the fact that neither Bobby Darin (my mother) nor John Holt (my father) were ever mentioned, served to betray the illegitimacy of their musical preferences as much as my hair, bottom and skin represented markers of an undesirable embodied capital within that school (Bourdieu 1986). Like the parents in the Black Middle Classes project, school became a 'site of constant battle for survival in terms of gaining recognition of one's racial identity as legitimate, let alone...a place to learn' (Rollock et al. 2011). In becoming racialised within this very specific classed and gendered context, I was beginning to see the world through a different space that I would later understand as 'the margins.'

Yet interestingly during my adult years, I would come to be perversely appreciative of my femininity recognising it as a considerable advantage relative, for example, to the emasculating experiences of my Black male counterparts. Yet there seems to be no place within the academy for my *Black femininity*. I have come to recognise that when white colleagues speak about feminism they do so placing an unspoken Whiteness at the normative centre of their analyses. No mention is made of race or racism. I am continually made invisible. And I would come to recognise that while my transition to middle classness facilitated access to the many spaces dominated by the white middle classes, when white colleagues speak about their class identification there remains scant acknowledgement of how their raced identity shapes a reading of a class identity that, depending on context, is informed differently from the middle classed experiences of other ethnic groups and remains supported by uninterrogated and presumptuous discourses of privilege and power.

I offer these reflections as a way of attending to the various ways in which I came to be and remain at the margins of educational spaces that are marked by intersecting forms of class and race discrimination (as well as inequalities of gender). I came to understand during my (private) schooling that I was an *inside outsider*, 'part of the whole but outside the main body' (hooks 1990, 149). This positioning has remained throughout my career in the academy. For all my class advantage, it is the colour of my skin to which others continue to react with fear, hesitation and intrigue requiring me, therefore, to constantly develop complex forms of *strategising for survival*; acts to which much of WhiteWorld (Gillborn 2008, 162) is completely oblivious.

Survival within the liminal space of alterity

In the section that follows I make use of one of the central tools of Critical Race Theory, story-telling (or counter-narrative) to highlight instances of marginality, resistance and agency within the racial justice project as played out within the academy. Counter-narrative can be semi-autobiographical or fictional in nature and acts as a powerful way for minoritised groups to creatively introduce concepts and arguments aimed at subverting and challenging the normative narratives of the dominant group (Delgado 2000; Delgado and Stefancic 2001). As with *The True Story* described above, I both tell the narrative and, simultaneously, speak back to the reader by interweaving an ongoing analysis and critical reflection of the events as they unfold.

In *The Counter-narrative*, I continue the story of Jonathan, a fictional Black academic working at a prestigious UK university, and chart his experiences as he attempts to successfully navigate his way through a higher education system in which he witnesses few Black academic staff in senior positions (ECU 2009; HEFCE 2008) and an ever increasing number taking their employer to tribunal. I first introduced Jonathan, and his partner Soray, in a paper discussing the concept of racial microaggressions (Rollock forthcoming). Both are composite characters in that they reflect actions and experiences from multiple sources. Both are Black and possess a critical awareness of the various ways in which their racialised identities are (mis) used by dominant others.

Part II – the counter-narrative

The wind howls miserably, shaking the fragile windows of the office. The building is deserted, bar a few security personnel and doctoral students committed to working late into the cold, dark night. Jonathan looks at his watch and sighs, promising himself that he will answer just one more email before heading home. He glances back at his inbox and notices that a new email has arrived. It's from the journal to which, at Soray's insistence, he had eventually submitted his most recent article. His eyes scan the email, voraciously searching for the key sentence that will let him know whether or not he had worked in vain:

'I am pleased to accept your paper for publication subject to your addressing the revisions detailed by the three reviewers. Their comments are attached.'

He relaxes momentarily, not realising how intensely he has been peering at the screen and then double clicks on the attachment. He muses how hesitant he had been about naming so explicitly microaggressions as an issue with which the academy had to contend. 'Outstanding contribution to the field...'[8] states the first reviewer. Jonathan smiles and nods to himself, satisfied. His eyes flit over the rest of the glowing review before he turns to the remarks of the second reviewer: 'The author offers an insightful and important theoretical analysis....' Jonathan exhales with relief, his smile broadening. He just didn't think the paper for all its theoretical sensitivies would be readily embraced. Soray had, in retrospect been correct about writing about his experiences, he reflects. He scans the comments of the final reviewer:

'The first thing I should say is that even though I am a white male those who know me will testify to my commitment to the types of diversity issues described in this paper.... While the paper has the potential to make an important contribution to the journal, the use of story-telling is simplistic and anecdotal.... I recommend that the author resubmits the paper using a more conventional methodology...'

Jonathan reads the comments again, more slowly this time and then, for reasons he cannot immediately articulate, he starts to laugh.

And he is still laughing when he switches off the light to his office, locks the door and begins the cold, long journey home.

Jonathan studied the young Black woman perched eagerly before him on the edge of his spare office chair. He saw it as part of his duty to 'give back' to his community by taking the time to share his experiences and give advice especially to any serious-minded Black person who was interested in becoming an academic or doing a further degree. He sighed inwardly knowing that such time and contributions were precisely the type of activity that wouldn't be acknowledged through any of the internal workload assessment procedures nor through the forthcoming REF[9] even though he was supporting the professional development of the next generation of Black and minority ethnic academics. And heavens knew the academy's record on progressing and retaining Black academics was far from impressive.

This particular woman Sandra (28-years-old, married with a young child) was considering registering to read for a PhD. A white colleague who had supervised Sandra through her Master's programme, had directed her to him adding in the email that Sandra 'might benefit from your particular knowledge and experience.' Having read a copy of her dissertation, Jonathan had been sufficiently impressed by her level of critical engagement with the literature on race theory to agree to an initial meeting.

'I'm sorry,' Sandra repeated, 'I know you're extremely busy. It's just I could really do with your advice. I have no idea of what doing a PhD entails. I would have spoken with Diana but...well.... I didn't find her very supportive when I was doing my MA. I don't feel she really knows anything about the subject area or understood the issues I was trying to examine. And I'd really appreciate your help about how best to become an academic.'

Sighing inwardly for a second time, Jonathan removed his glasses and uncrossed his legs. He looked at her and sighed again before finally asking: 'Tell me why you want a career in the academy.'

'I want to challenge some of the rubbish that is being published about us, about Black people and I think I can make a real difference through doing research and teaching and...'

'You need to write,' he interrupted, now only half-listening to her. 'You need to make sure your work is out there in the best journals.... He trailed off dismayed by his own simplicity as he remembered the feedback about his paper that he'd read just the night before. The reviewer's need to clumsily name his acceptance and understanding of 'diversity' (although Jonathan had himself never used that word in the paper) had been made all the more facile by the recommendation that he abandon his theoretical approach, steeped as it was in Critical Race Theory, and adopt a more 'conventional' model. Thank goodness that the other two reviewers had been unequivocal in their praise otherwise the paper would have been rejected altogether leaving him with the option of submitting elsewhere or, quite possibly and horrifically, accepting the reviewer's advice. He shuddered at the thought.

A career in the academy? He recalled his first UK conferences. Soul-destroying spaces of isolation with barely a visible Black face. He noticed how papers that covered race and racism tended to elicit the same steady set of unsophisticated, poorly thought-out questions about the role of absent (read: 'deficient') fathers, about social class, about the influence of peers on Black children's educational attainment, about the perceived lack of parental involvement. Following his first presentation about the Black middle classes and the racism that affected their lives despite their class position, an internationally renowned white Professor had put up his hand and, smiling with apparent conviviality, remarked how similar Jonathan's findings were to his own work on the white working classes, 'Surely this is just about difference and issues of belonging' he'd said, presenting his words as more of a statement than a question. Others in the audience had murmured and nodded in relieved consent at these words that offered welcome and easy escape from their own complicity in the various acts of racism that Jonathan had presented to them.

Such reactions to ignore the role of Whiteness and trivialise or altogether obliterate the possibility of racism can be understood as one of the many tools of Whiteness. Picower's (2009, 205) analyses of the ways in which her white students use such tools to maintain their hegemonic understanding of their racialised normalities is particularly apt here:

> ...[the] tools of Whiteness facilitate in the job of maintaining and supporting hegemonic stories and dominant ideologies of race, which in turn, uphold structures of White Supremacy. In an attempt to preserve their hegemonic understandings, participants [i.e. her students] used these tools to deny, evade, subvert, or avoid the issues raised. (emphasis added)

Within the context of higher education these acts of Whiteness, exemplified in the dismissive words of the renowned Professor, work to create and maintain what Delgado Bernal and Villalpando (2002, 169) call an 'apartheid of knowledge' that serves to 'marginalise, discredit and devalue the scholarship, epistemologies and other cultural resources of faculty of color.' We can understand, therefore, the challenge facing Jonathan. Even though he is presenting information gleaned from a serious qualitative study of the Black middle classes, the findings pertaining to racism and their racially minoritised status are alien and uncomfortable to his white colleagues. Committed to seeing the world through the lens of Whiteness they, like Picower's students find ways, albeit steeped in what appears to be civilised academic discourse, to deny the validity of his work and thus maintain this epistemological apartheid. Jonathan is presented with a challenge: how should he respond to such persistent acts of denial and still remain truthful to the data and his own experiences?

> Back then, he hadn't known how to react. Now he understood this as part of the complexity of Whiteness as white colleagues worked to protect their positions of privilege, worked to deny the presence of racism and trivialised his

research findings and, by implication, his experience and those of his research participants. 'Everyone is implicated in denial,' a white male colleague who he had thought understood the issues had stated during a discussion about the subject over lunch one afternoon, 'everyone is complicit. Even you,' he chuckled seemingly bemused by his own cleverness, 'are complicit by working in the academy as a Black male.' Jonathan had said nothing, pretending to give the statement serious consideration while chewing slowly on the remnants of his sandwich. In reality, he had been incensed at the way in which his colleague had sought to position as similar their experiences of the academy and, through wilful colour-blindness, disregard (his) white privilege and render Jonathan's racially minoritised experiences insignificant.

Sara Ahmed's (2009, 41) statement, about the complexities of embodying diversity when in a mainly white organisation, is apt here. She astutely reflects: 'if only we had the power we are imagined to possess, if only our proximity could be such a force. If only our arrival was their undoing (...). The argument is too much to sustain when your body is so exposed.' I want to situate these various forms of Whiteness, as demonstrated by the fictional white male Professor, the white others at the conference and Jonathan's lunch colleague, and the consequences they impose on our bodies as a *faux niceness* or *violence as niceness*. In the academy, such acts are often presented under the guise of 'polite' collegiality and theoretical debate while the 'violence' they impose on academics of colour, denying and subjugating their experience, remains unnoticed. It is precisely this white investment in niceness that contributes to what Leonardo and Porter (2010) describe as the myth of 'safe racial dialogue.' In other words, those conversations about race that feel comfortable and safe for whites are, in fact, fraught with tension and difficulty for racially minoritised groups who attempt genuine race dialogue but are consistently confronted by what might be described as a *Whiteness as default* positioning. Leonardo and Porter contend that while 'violence' in this context might be conceptualised as 'euphemized,' it is nonetheless damaging, serving to maintain 'links between material distributions of power and a politics of recognition, and lowers standards of humanity' (2010, 140). It is the complex *nano*-politics of these very issues that trouble Jonathan as he considers what advice he might be able to give to a student of colour interested in pursuing a career in the academy:

> Should he really tell this young woman sat before him to drop everything to become an academic? What should he tell her: that she could change it from within? Hadn't he learnt the hard way how embedded the systems of Whiteness were? Wouldn't she be better off working in the private sector where although they weren't bound by race equalities legislation she could ultimately earn enough money to enable her to make the choices she needed regarding the schooling of her young child?

'Er. . .yes, I need to write. Is there anything else?' the young woman asked, looking slightly concerned at Jonathan's apparent lapse in concentration. 'Is there anything else I need to do?'

Jonathan's sigh was audible this time. Rising to his feet, he clasped his hands behind his back and paced, deep in thought, to the window that overlooked the university car park below. 'Was she ready?' he wondered, 'Could he trust that she would understand?'

'Yes, there is something else you need to do but. . .' he turned, ready to study her reaction, 'it won't be easy.'

Sandra looked at him expectantly but without the bafflement he had anticipated. Moderately reassured he returned to his desk and identified the folder saved on his computer as 'In Progress.' His eyes scanned the various documents he had saved within it until he found what he was looking for. He paused momentarily, fingers hovering over the keyboard, before entering the password that he had set up to protect the file from any prying eyes and printed the document that finally presented itself to him.

Retrieving the article from the printer he looked down at it, feeling slightly protective of the words that he had written there.

'Here, take this,' he shoved the sheet awkwardly in her direction, keen to have her take it before he changed his mind, 'go away, have a read and if you still want to pursue an academic career get back in touch with me. We can talk then. . .but you must keep this to yourself. Keep what's written there confidential. . .'

Sandra nodded and stood, conscious that the meeting was being brought to a close. Slightly confused by the entire exchange, she accepted the paper from Jonathan's outstretched hand, only able to glance briefly at it as she gathered her coat and bag.

'Oh and it's not quite finished,' Jonathan added, as she made to leave the room.

'Um. . .that's okay. Thank you so much for your time.' As she closed the door behind her, Sandra paused and read the heading on the paper she had been handed. In bold, black text at the top of the page stood the words: *Rules of Racial Engagement for (Possible) Survival in WhiteWorld.*

The rules that follow can be understood as part of what I am defining as the racially minoritised habitus. Although I do not attempt to suggest that every person who is racially minoritised considers their experiences or strategizes in precisely this way it should be borne in mind that the kind of micro-analysis and strategizing that will be revealed shortly in the rules was also reflected in the experiences of many of the Black middle class parents in the ESRC project mentioned earlier. Clearly such thinking is not unusual to those within this group. For example, in the following extract Ella (Senior Management, Health Sector) discusses the tactics she employs to manage incidents where she has been racially othered:

> I think it is very very difficult (...) you are going to drop the voice, (...); you are going to try to talk round it. You try and say look this is why and give an explanation. You have to try not to be angry, you know, it is very difficult but you have to...the worst thing you can show is anger right, because then it is all gone, because then you are so obviously the aggressor [in their eyes]. If you try to be calm in dealing with the situation, 'problem-solve' [says this slowly and deliberately, slightly scornful, using her fingers to denote that problem-solving is in quotes]. I am going to work it out with you. We are professionals. I am not going to be emotive about it even though it is a painfully emotive experience. I have got to lose that and I have got to deal with this situation as a problem-solving thing. It means I think that it affects your personality because it means in other situations you tend not to be overly assertive, so that you are not seen in other situations as an aggressor, therefore when you deal with things like this they can look at the rest of your personality, and although they want to label you as an aggressor now it doesn't quite fit the rest. So [it's] almost as if you mould yourself into a certain 'placid' individual (...)

What is difficult to reflect here is the tone with which Ella conveyed the above. Her pace was steady, careful, precise. She is clearly recounting experiences and strategies with which she is extremely familiar. She was calm but also sounded both bemused and weary as she detailed the amount of extra work and energy required to defend one's identity from insult while simultaneously remaining alert to white sensitivities about race. And I would go further to suggest that she is also disappointed by continued white denial. Fatigue, bemusement and disappointment are interwoven with undercurrents of condescension as she details the ways in which she is obliged to navigate and manage whites who remain oblivious to, yet complicit in, the complexities of the entire racialised situation. Ahmed (2009, 48) speaks to the personal consequences and challenges of this kind of nano-politicking when she acknowledges how being an outspoken Black feminist who highlights instances of racism or sexism can lead to her being positioned as a 'killjoy,' as a bringer of bad feeling to an otherwise (perceived) racially and sexually equitable and harmonious discussion. In presenting the 'Rules of Racial Engagement' I am seeking to summarise and name elements of this strategising and, in so doing, reveal the multilayered and nuanced analysis required for survival by those in the margins.

Rules of Racial Engagement for (Possible) Survival in WhiteWorld[10]

1 Avoid directly or even in passing accusing whites of racism, even if you believe their words or actions to be horrendously racist or racially Othering.

This sends whites in a frenzy of guilt; denial; anger so that they are no longer able to engage in conversation and rather than hearing or understanding the point you are making, you will become positioned as the aggressor or killjoy.

2 On matters concerning race be prepared to 'problem-solve,' engage, negotiate.

In other words act as though you are simply exploring some abstract idea or a suggestion in a professionally engaging manner. This presents you as non-challenging and reasonable and keeps whites 'safe' in feeling that the issues of race inequity being discussed have absolutely nothing to do with them – even though they do. This is a challenging rule for those committed to the racial justice project. The aim is to encourage change, disrupt the status quo, which requires some level of white discomfort. Yet when is it safe for us to make whites uncomfortable?

Be careful with this rule – you need to maintain the pseudo-safety of the dialogue but also challenge restrictive thinking while keeping your sanity intact. Support mechanisms are crucial. [see # 10]

3 Maintain a lowered tone of voice in debates on race, especially where there is a difference of opinion.

The aim is to always seem reasonable and friendly. Use a raised tone with care even if you have been deeply insulted.

4 Be prepared.

Whites will trivialise and position as anecdotal accounts of racism. Be prepared for this by knowing your subject area. Have countless sources of evidence and supporting examples. Statistics are always helpful. [Note: Qualitative evidence is likely to be refuted and closely questioned]. When writing for publication rigorously ground your analysis in theory. Good use of theory can provide a pathway to some form of academic legitimacy, albeit tenuous.

5 Don't show emotion or keep to a 'safe' minimum. Definitely don't show anger.

This is especially important for Black men but applies equally to Black women. Like the raised voice [see #3] use emotion strategically and with care.

Sometimes well-placed emotion, supported by a number of sources of evidence, can be highly effective. Do not overuse this strategy; emotion (irrespective of its appropriateness to the context) is not a license readily available to persons of colour.

6 Work at all times at presenting a friendly and reasonable persona.

This is a central tactic. If you work to present an image as friendly and approachable this will give you some degree of license, since it will seem out of character, to deploy a raised voice and emotion to your advantage should the circumstance warrant it.

7 Employ the 'language of Whiteness' to make your case.

Understand the strength of language as a unifying tactic. Begin discussions and debates with words, phrases, examples and points of reference that whites will understand and relate to. Only then attempt to demonstrate differences that are to do with race and racism. Never be complacent or underestimate the power of Whiteness as default positioning. Always be prepared for the fact that they may never understand the full extent of issues pertaining to racism.

8 Dress and carry yourself in a 'non-threatening' manner.

In your professional capacity never risk wearing clothes or items that whites might use to misread or confuse your class position and subjugate you even more. Your class position can be used as some minimal yet fragile *protection against certain forms of racism.*[11]

9 Be on your guard.

Acts of Othering and microaggression surface in the most unexpected ways, at unexpected times and are not restricted simply to those conversations that centre explicitly on race.[12]

10 Develop and nurture sacred spaces and protected narratives.

Work to ensure a strong support network comprising of white allies, Black colleagues and friends. This network will act as your sacred space of sanctity where there is minimal or no need for the Rules of Racial Engagement. Such spaces provide an opportunity to engage in forms of narrative protected from the dehumanizing violence of WhiteWorld. These are narratives with which to theorise, decode, de-stress in relative safety and to reaffirm one's humanity.

These rules can be considered as a template for survival or possible survival within mainly white spaces. I do not suggest the list is complete. Indeed Jonathan notes that it is a work in progress yet there is much within them that speaks to the tensions and apparent contradictions of attempting to survive in that space at the margins. I explore these issues further in the following section.

Dismantling discourses of Whiteness

Black folks coming from poor, underclass [sic] communities, who enter universities or privileged community settings unwilling to surrender every vestige of who we were before we were there, all 'sign' of our class and cultural 'difference,' who are willing to play the role of 'exotic Other,' must create spaces within that culture of domination if we are to survive whole, our souls intact. (hooks 1990, 148)

In devising a set of strategies for survival, my fictional character Jonathan is both recognising and naming the contours of his own existence as racially marginalised and simultaneously revealing the ways in which Whiteness operates, in quite violent ways, to remain at the normative centre. Even while he comprehends this, his broader commitment to race equality and a personal need for a humanizing existence, necessitates that he finds ways to disrupt the white status quo while at the same time endeavouring to remain vigilant of the ever-ready sensitivities of whites who refuse to name and critically reflect on their place in the manifestation of White Supremacy. There are risks involved in 'outing' not seeing whites, in naming the contours of Whiteness, that could make the difference between a paper being accepted or not accepted by a journal, that could affect the ways in which others engage with his research and thus his capacity to advance his career. This reflects just one aspect of the awkward oscillating tension between liminality as advantageous and liminality as disadvantageous. To what extent does employing the 'language of Whiteness,' a phrase borrowed from a parent in the Black Middle Classes project, while a clever unifying strategy to gain the ear of whites in fact obfuscate the objectives of the racial justice project? What are the conditions under which one is able to make more explicit the goals of the project and reduce or ultimately discard such strategising?

Leonardo and Porter (2010) argue that in order to move towards racial justice there will invariably be some discomfort for those at the centre as they edge with resistance towards the recognition of their own investment in and endorsement of racism. I want further to argue that while such discomfort may be a necessary part of the move towards racial equity, it also represents a point of instability and danger for those of colour if whites fear that their positions of privilege and power are under threat or even merely being called into question. This, indisputably, is a serious consideration within the many spaces where whites are the gatekeepers or hold power in terms of decision-making (Collins 1991; Leonardo 2002). There are also countless additional matters to consider. Steer too far in the direction of disrupting Whiteness and Jonathan is likely to be construed as an aggressor or killjoy. Any future arguments or standpoints he presents will be deemed irrational, overly emotive and ultimately thwart his attempts to advance racial justice. Maintain too closely the 'nice safety' of the racial dialogue and he becomes one of the not seeing, complicit in the very practices he seeks to disrupt. He becomes further dehumanized seemingly unable to escape from what Fanon (1967, 88) evocatively describes as a kind of 'infernal circle.'

In drawing together different strands of analyses – counter-narrative, autobiography, data analysis – I have sought to reveal precisely the extent of the highly strategic and careful analyses required by those in the margins who are able to see. These tensions and negotiations demonstrate the extra work required for the person of colour within white society. Such work can, without contradiction, be conceptualised both as an implicit requirement to survive Whiteness and as an agentic critical response to it. I have demonstrated that power, status, gender and context interact in multiple sometimes opposing ways to lend a complexity to the experiences and very being of those persons of colour who work to advance the racial justice project even while race is becoming more embedded, more nuanced, thus necessitating increasingly sophisticated strategies for survival (Ladson-Billings 1998).

Earlier I described, borrowing from Zeus Leonardo, the need within the racial justice project to name, reflect on and dismantle discourses of Whiteness. In presenting the arguments in this article I have sought to add my voice from the 'radical space of my marginality' (hooks 1990, 151) to the numerous others engaged in the same fight towards racial justice (e.g. Crenshaw 1989; hooks 1990; Bell 1992; Ladson-Billings1998; Delgado 2000).

I am talking back and working towards disrupting Whiteness.

Afterword

Extract from Jonathan's diary – Sacred Spaces and Protected Narratives

It is a barren terrain, the lands stretch for indeterminable distance, tumble weeds scatter in the wind. Sometimes in this dry land you encounter others like you, searching for a place, an island of comfort where we can rest, where we can take off the masks and be at one with the person crying with pain beneath the veil. This is a place where we can nurse the cuts, the grazes, the wounds that run deep.... And even when we encounter those others we have to still assess their trustworthiness. Can we really take the mask off with them? If we can, we sit on dry, unyielding land and share stories. We find others who recognise the pain. We create sacred spaces that are for us only us. We throw off the oppressive language and embodiment of WhiteWorld and intersperse our speech with colloquialisms, with the tongues of our mother countries and, for a brief precious moment, we relax. We shake our heads, hold each other's hands, we sigh, deep, deep sighs that only we and our ancestors can hear and engage in our protected narratives...narratives we keep protected from WhiteWorld. We laugh at the skill, at the strategising, at the recognition of some WhiteWorld act that we each have come to know only too well but of which WhiteWorld is oblivious...or unconcerned – caught up as it is in perpetuating the status quo. And we gain a temporary strength – for 'tis only temporary – as we stand, stretch our limbs, dust off our clothes and continue on our journey, leaving behind promises to meet again in this Sacred Space.

Acknowledgment

I would like to thank Gregg Beratan, Jide Fadipe and David Gillborn for their helpful comments on an earlier draft of this paper.

Notes

1. Economic & Social Research Council (RES-062-23-1880). I am carrying out this project with Professors Carol Vincent, Stephen Ball and David Gillborn.
2. Critical Race Theory recognises that racism is endemic and embedded as a normal part of the way in which society functions.
3. Lucy's name is a pseudonym as are those used in relation to the Black Middle Classes project.
4. A 'well-heeled,' relatively affluent area of south-west London.
5. Caran d'Ache is a Swiss based company specialising in writing instruments. According to their website: 'In that area of emotions where writing and images fuse together, graceful shapes, vigorous lines and deep colours create the passion that Caron d'Ache has for Fine Writing.' Only certain girls (white, middle class) owned these pencils. They were presented in flat, Caron D'Ache presentation box sets of 30 to 40 coloured pencils – 'the first water-soluble colour pencil since 1931' – that when dipped in water produced an effect not dissimilar to water paints. www.carandache.ch/m/les-instruments-d-ecriture-et-accessoires/index.lbl (last accessed 15 November 2010).
6. Preparatory schools are independent schools that prepare young children for continued (usually secondary) education in fee-paying schools.
7. Dill and Zambrana (2009, 4) define Intersectionality as a framework that examines the 'relationships and interactions between multiple axes of identity and multiple dimensions of social organization – at the same time.' Intersectionality is particularly useful as a means of reframing and creating new ways of studying power and inequality and challenging traditional modes of thinking about marginalised groups.
8. All of the reviews are entirely fictional.
9. The Research Excellence Framework is a process through which the quality of the research work of academics and UK higher education institutions is assessed. This is a highly competitive process which sees financial rewards attached to the highest university outcomes. http://www.hefce.ac.uk/research/ref/ (accessed 11 November 2010)
10. I am grateful to and have been inspired by the work of Derrick Bell, one of the key proponents of Critical Race Theory, who in a chapter entitled 'The Rules of Racial Standing' emphasizes some of the contradictions evident when in naming racism as a problem in a society where whites continue to deny its existence (Bell 1992).
11. See Rollock et al. (2011).
12. For example, see Rollock (2011).

References

Ahmed, S. 2009. Embodying diversity: Problems and paradoxes for black feminists. *Race Ethnicity and Education* 12, no. 1: 41–52.

Bell, D. 1992. *Faces at the bottom of the well: The permanence of racism.* New York: Basic Books.

Bourdieu, P. 1984. *Distinction: A social critique of the judgement of taste.* New York and London: Routledge.

Bourdieu, P. 1986. The forms of capital. In *Handbook of theory of research for the sociology of education,* ed. J.E. Richardson, 241–58. New York: Greenwood Press.

Collins, P. 1991. *Black feminist thought: Knowledge, consciousness, and the politics of empowerment.* 2nd ed. New York and London: Routledge.

Crenshaw, K. 1989. Mapping the margins: Intersectionality, identity politics and violence against women of color. In *Critical race theory: The key writings that formed the movement*, ed. K. Crenshaw, N. Gotanda, G. Peller, and K. Thomas, 357–84. New York: The New Press.

Delgado, R. 2000. Storytelling for oppositionists and others: A plea for narrative. In *Critical race theory: The cutting edge*, 2nd ed., ed. R. Delgado and J. Stefancic, 60–70. Philidelphia, PA: Temple University Press.

Delgado, R., and J. Stefancic. 2001. *Critical race theory: An introduction*. New York and London: New York University Press.

Delgado, B.D., and O. Villalpando. 2002. An apartheid of knowledge in academia: The struggle over the "legitimate" knowledge of faculty of color. *Equity & Excellence in Education* 35, no. 2: 169–80.

Dill, B.T., and R.E. Zambrana. 2009. *Emerging intersections: Race, class and gender in theory, policy and practice*. New Brunswick, NJ: Rutgers University Press.

Ellison, R. 1965. *The invisible man*. London: Penguin Books.

Equality Challenge Unit. 2009. *Equality in higher education: Statistical report 2009*. London: ECU.

Fanon, F. 1967 [2008]. *Black skin white masks*. Exeter: Pluto Press.

Gillborn, D. 2005. Education policy as an act of white supremacy: Whiteness, critical race theory and education reform. *Journal of Educational Policy* 20: 485–505.

Gillborn, D. 2008. *Racism and education: Coincidence or conspiracy?* London: Routledge.

Higher Education Funding Council for England. 2008. *Staff employed at HEFCE-funded HEIs: Update*. Bristol: HEFCE.

hooks, b. 1990. *Yearning: Race, gender and cultural politics*. Toronto, Ontario: Between the Lines.

Ladson-Billings, G. 1998. Just what is critical race theory and what's it doing in a nice field like education? *International Journal of Qualitative Studies in Education* 11, no. 1: 7–24.

Ladson-Billings, G., and J. Donnor. 2008. The moral activist role of critical race theory scholarship. In *The landscape of qualitative research*, ed. N.K. Denzin and Y.S. Lincoln, 279–301. Los Angeles, CA: Sage Publications.

Leonardo, Z. 2002. The souls of white folk: Critical pedagogy, whiteness studies, and globalization discourse. *Race Ethnicity and Education* 5, no. 1: 29–50.

Leonardo, Z., and R.K. Porter. 2010. Pedagogy of fear: Toward a Fanonian theory of 'safety' in race dialogue. *Race Ethnicity and Education* 13, no. 2: 139–58.

McIntosh, P. 1997. White privilege and male privilege: A personal account of coming to see correspondences through work in women's studies. In *Critical white studies: Looking behind the mirror*, ed. R. Delgado and J. Stefancic, 291–9. Philadelphia, PA: Temple University Press.

Picower, B. 2009. The unexamined whiteness of teaching: How white teachers maintain and enact dominant racial ideologies. *Race Ethnicity and Education* 12, no. 2: 197–215.

Rollock, N. 2011. Unspoken rules of engagement: Navigating racial microaggressions in the academic terrain. *International Journal of Qualitative Studies in Education* February. DOI:10.1080/09518398.2010.543433.

Rollock, N., D. Gillborn, C. Vincent, and S. Ball. 2011. The public identities of the black middle classes: Managing race in public spaces. *Sociology* 45, no. 6: 1078–93.

Tate IV, W.F. 1997. Critical race theory and education: History, theory, and implications. *Review of Research in Education* 22: 195–247.

Wildman, S.M., with A.D. Davis. 1997. Making systems of privilege visible. In *Critical white studies: Looking behind the mirror*, ed. R. Delgado and J. Stefancic, 314–19. Philadelphia, PA: Temple University Press.

Wynter, S. 1992. *Do not call us Negros: How 'multicultural' textbooks perpetuate racism*. San Francisco, CA: Aspire Books.

Rediscovering 'Race Traitor': towards a Critical Race Theory informed public pedagogy

John Preston and Charlotte Chadderton

This article attempts to politically resituate Ignatiev and Garvey's conception of the 'Race Traitor' within contemporary notions of Critical Race Theory and Public Pedagogy. Race Traitor has been critiqued both by those on the academic and neo-conservative right, who accuse advocates of the project of genocide and misuse of public funds, and has a number of critics on the left who consider that the project is misguided, posturing and self-affirming for guilty whites and politically untenable. There are also post-structuralist critiques of the 'Race Traitor' position, which overstate its focus on embodiment and the post-racial as opposed to its concrete suggestions for resisting racial oppression. In this article we argue that Race Traitor must be situated within the politics of its time, which is within anarchist and Marxist politics, and that this contextualisation enables one to consider Race Traitor as a political form with resonance for contemporary Marxists, Anarchists and in struggles against racial oppression. Ignatiev and Garvey's manifesto, that 'treason to whiteness is loyalty to humanity,' still has resonance amongst some anarchist groups both in the UK and North America. 'Race Traitor' has since been propagated through more recent work in Critical Race Theory by writers such as Derek Bell (an early reader of the 'Race Traitor' material), Richard Delgado and Zeus Leonardo, and we argue that Critical Race Theory provides a useful corrective to claims that a white autonomous movement can resist racial oppression. The article concludes by considering how CRT and public pedagogy may produce new political praxis for Race Traitors in the twenty-first century.

Introduction

The purpose of this article is to consider the relevance of Noel Ignatiev's Race Traitor (RT) project as a strategy to fight racial oppression in England. As capitalist discourse and neoliberal forms of governance penetrate more aspects of our lives, as inequalities grow, as public spaces and spaces for resistance are being dismantled, this article is situated in the context of our ongoing search for theories which offer a realistic alternative and consideration of the options for building collective resistance.

As we explain in the body of the article, Anarchist and Marxist movements, in both Europe and the US, which might offer a workable alternative to neoliberalism, have tended to be deracialised. In this article, we rediscover the historical and theoretical links between the RT project, Marxist thinking, Anarchist theory and Critical Race Theory (CRT) in order to consider the possible role – if any at all - white people can play in the fight against racial oppression. A public pedagogy of activism (Sandlin, Schultz, and Burdick 2010), informed by insights from CRT and RT, would seem to offer a possible way forward. The notion of a public pedagogy is seen as a useful and radical option for activism because it is aimed at pedagogical activity in the public sphere, examining popular cultural forms as sites of learning and also taking direct political action to be a site of pedagogy and politics. This can include activities such as culture jamming (Sandlin and Milam 2010), protest (Ayers 2010) and community action (Stovall 2010). Moreover, public pedagogy has started to reclaim the methodological space of the critical pedagogue (or demagogue!) through redefining praxis for public intellectuals.

Situating the situationists: the political origins of Race Traitor

Noel Ignatiev's (formally known as Ignatin) Race Traitor project is in need of recontextualisation, in terms of its past and its potential future as a strategy to fight racial oppression in its contemporary form as globalised white supremacy in North America and Europe. This need for recontextualisation is threefold. Firstly, Race Traitor is accused by contemporary critics of being fascist and individualised, despite having an intimate history with Marxist, anarchist and black radical politics. Secondly, in critiques based around whiteness and embodiment, Race Traitor is accused of being post-racial, whereas in actuality the objectives of Race Traitor are towards a society free of racial oppression rather than one where whites are free of 'whiteness.' Thirdly, we argue that the Race Traitor project could usefully be updated by taking on critiques from Critical Race Theory and adopting methodologies of public pedagogy.

'Race Traitor' is a contested term. The term did not suddenly appear with the work of Noel Ignatiev on the abolition of whiteness. According to Zack 'Race Traitor' was initially used by white Americans in the Southern US for whites who supported black demands for civil rights (Zack 1999 quoted in Kannen 2008). However, it was also used in various ways in the US in the 1930s to describe 'treasonous' positions with regard to race of various kinds. In 1934 (in a column by Ralph Matthews in the *Afro American*, 24th November), for example, a white factory owner who did not support equal rights for African American workers was described as a 'race traitor' to the interests of African Americans as opposed to a 'race champion.' The term was also applied to a Jewish woman arrested in

Bavaria for '...having intimate relations with an Aryan man' (*Lewiston Evening Journal*, 16th November 1935). In these cases, 'race traitor' is described in moral or political terms, and the term has different meanings according to historical context and the political orientation of the writer. In the contemporary context, the term is, for example, widely propagated by extreme white supremacist groups (such as Stormfront) who use the term 'race traitor' for those (and they are legion) who show disloyalty to their esoteric and fascist conception of whiteness. In terms of its etymology, then, the term has circulated broadly with many different associations in different media.

Due to this linguistic pluralism it is important to distinguish RT ('Race Traitor') as a political movement from its use in popular parlance where it can have a variety of meanings in terms of orientation to whiteness, blackness, Anti-Semitism and more generally racial 'passing' with both positive and negative connotations. Clear definition of even RT itself is further complicated as RT is not a coherent political movement in the sense of party, federation or grouping and it draws upon various political philosophies. It exists as a journal, website and a very loose political federation of activists and, befitting its nature, is autonomous in that it doesn't have a centrally organised structure.

Although Noel Ignatiev is sometimes called the 'architect' of RT, he is actually responsible for bringing together various strands of activism and political thought. The journal RT and the book (Ignatiev and Garvey 1996) considers that the US (and by implication other capitalist societies such as the UK) are white supremacist and that capitalism hinges on the maintenance of white hegemony. The task of individuals, or groups of RTs, is to 'abolish the white race' through treasonous acts. These treasonous acts to whiteness are not codifiable but have to be seen in a historical context, so that acts that may seem trivial now can be seen to be radical in their historical context and vice-versa (Ignatiev and Garvey 1996). Although RT does not seek a firm definition of the treasonous act, it gives a variety of examples from the physically violent, such as initiating a prison riot or attacking fascists, through protests and direct action to verbal acts of defiance. Acts of race treason can very often unleash violence against the traitor: verbal and symbolic but very often physical: indicative of the very violence that keeps white racial bonding intact.

The focus of RT on action rejects the romantic idealisation of the 'exceptional white' and considers that treasonous acts rather than individual actors should be the subject of discussion. However, although treasonous acts cannot be grouped, there are two common features of the treasonous acts described in RT. Firstly, they break with white racial bonding. White supremacy is so pervasive that it is not possible to serve the desires of an existing white constituency: 'We are calling for the opposite. A minority willing to undertake outrageous acts of provocation, aware that they will incur the opposition of many who might agree with them if they adopted a more moderate approach' (Ignatiev and Garvey 1996, 36). Secondly, that they are anti-statist or anti-capitalist in nature. It is not possible for a treasonous act to be initiated from within the state or capitalist enterprises '. . .the main target of those who seek to eradicate the color line should be the institutions that maintain it: the schools, the criminal justice and welfare systems, the employers and unions and the family' (Ignatiev and Garvey 1996, 180).

Fundamentally then, RT wishes to abolish whiteness as a form of privilege, which is alien to democratic social justice philosophies where equity is paramount and can be achieved through consensus and also alien to Marxist philosophies where the revolutionary overthrow of capital alone is important. The lack of stable referents for RT means that critics on both the left and right frequently position RT either as emerging from a position of anti-white fascism, or the quasi-fascist fantasising of an extreme liberal (Ignatiev) arguing that the RT position is, fundamentally, genocidal. These critiques, however, tend to be based on a misunderstanding of the notion of the abolition of whiteness, in which there is confusion over whiteness as a phenotype, and whiteness as a hegemonic structure, as will be explained below. The critics are primarily on the right although there is a left, Marxist, critique of the supposedly fascist nature of RT:

> Dr. Ignatiev has an idea like Hitler. A race is guilty and must go. The communists said that a guilty class had to go. If you thought that genocide was left behind in the 20th Century, be surprised that genocide has a home in the education system.' (Bruce 2004)

> '. . .the style in which Race Traitor's ideological position is written is worryingly reminiscent of Nazi propaganda. . .' (Cole 2009a: 33)

Reading these statements one might consider that RT emerges from an extreme Black Nationalist perspective (or a self destructive, self loathing white suicidal perspective) but these critiques are wilfully unaware of the historical and political context from which RT developed and confuse semiotics with reality. The charge of fascism, in particular, is often levelled at radical movements against racial oppression. For example, one may consider Marcus Garvey's Universal Negro Improvement Association (UNIA) in the early 1920s to be 'fascist' in the same way as Hitler (Gilroy 2000). Similarly, one may easily portray Marx to be 'racist' (Weyl 1979) if one took his comments on Jewish people, Mexican people and African Americans out of their historical context. Likewise, RT is a political form which must be located in the political movements of the late 1960s and the coalescing of political and practical philosophies at that time that emerged in an autonomist grouping calling itself the STO (Soujourner Truth Organisation). The language used and statements made therefore reflect its origins in and around 1968. RT certainly did not grow out of the imagination of Noel

Ignatiev alone, and was the antithesis of fascist politics (supporting the sorts of violent action against fascists now propagated by existing Anarchist groups such as the Anarchist Federation, London Class War and emergently Antifa - '…any action that aims to crush the Nazis physically and fails to do so because of state intervention has the effect of reinforcing the authority of the state, which, as we said, is the most important agency maintaining race barriers': Ignatiev and Garvey 1996, 181) but is not simply anti-fascist, having attachments to various other forms of Marxist, Anarchist and Black political movements. In particular, it owes its existence to the radical politics of W.E.B. Du Bois and Sojourner Truth as well as to other 1960s Black Power movements such as the (Maoist inspired) Black Panthers and the spin off, situationist 'White Panther Party.' Within 'New Left' movements such as the STO there was an understanding that Black political movements were the starting point for revolutionary activity: 'Those features which became the hallmarks of the New Left – the recognition that racism was not an iso-lated flaw, the focus on direct action, the internationalization of the struggle – all these took first shape [*sic*] in the movement of Black people' (Ignatiev 1980)

The Sojourner Truth Organisation (STO), a Marxist organisation, was indeed the genesis of the modern RT project. The STO considered that the existence of whiteness was the primary obstacle in bringing about a Com-munist revolution in the United States. Likewise Ignatiev considered that in any revolutionary project '…we should reject from the outset any approach involving a capitulation to white workers' sense of their distinctive interests as whites, which is the *main form of bourgeois consciousness and the main obstacle to the development of proletarian class consciousness among them*' (Ignatiev 1980, emphasis added). Ignatiev considers that white supremacy is an objective condition in the US: 'Everything in the U.S. must be viewed through the prism of the white supremacist contract on which bourgeois hegemony rests' (Ignatiev 1980). The autonomists considered that this strug-gle should be self directed and independent of trade unions or other political organisations in leading to working class revolution. The STO was a pre-dominantly white, grassroots, revolutionary organisation that prioritised pragmatism and local struggles as connected with wider political struggles. It stressed the importance of workplace organisation and many of its mem-bers subsequently worked in Detroit factories in the 1970s, agitating and organising wildcat strikes. The organisation published a range of publica-tions whose titles may seem to be passé today – a newspaper (*Insurgent Worker*), a theoretical journal (*Urgent Tasks*) and a series of discussion pam-phlets. These are informative in that they foreshadow the creation of the 'Race Traitor' political project within Marxist and Anarchist theory and foreshadow a break with reformist, statist, anti-racism. In 'Fighting Racism: An Exchange', for example, Ignatiev and Lynd (Ignatiev, Lynd, and Lawrence 1975) debate Lynd's proposal that rather than overturn white privilege and institutional racism white workers should aim for better housing, employment and wages for black workers. Ignatiev criticises this approach on two grounds. Firstly, the suggestion that a white intellectual, reformist project could change material conditions ignores the '...self directed activity of the black community' which is '...the *most significant anti-capitalist force*' (Ignatiev, Lynd, and Lawrence 1975, emphasis added). Secondly, Lynd considers that improving schooling for African Americans is a technical fix and ignores that for a graduate '...his school plays a part in guaranteeing him [*sic*] an edge over black folk in the labour market and that's all that he expects from it' (Ignatiev, Lynd, and Lawrence 1975). 'Gimmicky' reformist programmes are no substitute for '...the direct confrontation with the reactionary aspects of white workers' consciousness' (Ignatiev, Lynd, and Lawrence 1975). However, the matter is not simply one of combating false consciousness but also the structural and institutional supports for white supremacy which had led to '...the creation of a class of laborers whose community of interest with their supporters was legally and publically affirmed' (Ignatiev 1980). Abolishing whiteness, then, was a necessary step in bringing the US to the historical position where it could become a Communist society – a position that seems headily utopian and (perhaps less so given the current crisis of capitalism) unrealistic today, but in the discussions of the 1968 STO was a real historical possibility.

However, aside from a clear Marxist orientation, there is also an Anarchist turn to RT which makes it stand apart from municipal, or reformist, anti-racism. Like Anarchism more generally, RT is '...ultimately neither the subject of a pedagogy, nor the object of an ideology' (Acosta 2009), being an autonomist and unfolding political movement to abolish whiteness. Olson (2009, 35) considers that RT has resonance with existing anarchist groups such as Love and Rage, Anarchist People of Colour and Bring the Ruckus (to which one could add the English Anarchist groups London Class War and the Anarchist Federation, mentioned previously) although the Anarchist movement has been largely ignorant of Black Power and Black resistance '...Black freedom struggles have been the most revolutionary tradition in American history yet the anarchist milieu is all but unaware of it' (Olson 2009, 42). The Anarchist movements in America and England, particularly, have also been criticised for their lack of awareness of race with white anarchists being resistant to charges of 'white skin privilege' (Nomous 2001). Olson rails against this ideological rejection of white supremacy as a form of oppression and calls for a rethinking of RT in terms of an anarchist movement that foregrounds struggle against white supremacy, rather than a broad anti-racist front, through active resistance to the state institutions that maintain it, in particular the police and prisons, although this could be expanded to include schools and universities.

However, unlike other autonomist movements, RT is not concerned with the transcendence of whiteness but rather with its abolition as a category of racial oppression and would be opposed to anarchist writers (Bey 1991; Malott 2006) who consider, for example, that it is possible to transcend categories of power in the creation of Temporary Autonomous Zones (TAZ) where, albeit fleetingly, an insurrection may produce a situation of human freedom where existing power structures would not exist. Although the political realisation of being in a TAZ could provide further political strategies for overturning the structural conditions of whiteness, RT is concerned with the permanent abolition of whiteness as a societal and structural concern. I would therefore contend that RT has some contemporary relevance, particularly in its influence in the thinking of some Anarchist groups and, although it may be of some surprise to its contemporary Marxist critics (Cole 2009a, 2009b, 2009c, 2009d; Cole and Maisuria 2007) RT emerged from a situated working class autonomist–Marxist perspective on the relationship between capitalism and white supremacy. Autonomism was also clearly influenced by situationism and one can consider that part of RT is to disrupt the normal 'spectacle' of white privilege and supremacy in a situationist fashion. To identify it as 'fascist,' even in its rhetorical register (as Cole 2009a, 33), does so without contextualising RT within the nature of autonomist working class struggle, and its close association with Black political struggle, in the US post-WWII.

Is RT post-racial?

RT is sometimes caricatured by its critics as adopting a post-racial stance, whereby an individual, or even a community, is required to abolish their whiteness in the name of creating a world in which race no longer features. Such critiques argue that white people cannot *choose* not to be white and hence that such a choice is naïve, bizarre, insincere, reactionary and ultimately impossible. As stated above, such analyses decontextualise RT, misunderstanding the notion as being concerned with individual action rather than as part of an activist political movement. These critiques also tend to misunderstand the aim of RT as attempting to abolish whiteness as a phenotype, rather than as a hegemonic structure.

There are a number of different approaches to the critique of RT as post-racial. The first concerns the embeddedness of whiteness within other social structures and aspects of personhood. According to Levine-Rasky (2002) whiteness must be contextualised in order to understand how it operates across class fractions and that '*individual* acts' of resistance are those supported by the RT position (Levine-Rasky 2002 341, emphasis added). 'For race traitors, whiteness is nothing more than a false identity based on unjust practices and a collective conformity to a white exclusiveness' (Levine-Rasky 2002, 340). In this definition RT actions are seen to be about breaking with this conformity, which fails to recognise both the contextual elements of whiteness (in terms particularly of class, but also of gender) but also the 'deep investments' (339) that so-called whites and people of colour have in maintaining the racial order. However, it could be argued that these forms of contextualisation may actually enhance the RT position as white-ness is recontextualised by other social oppressions. So white positionality (whiteness) is informed by the multiple intersectionalities of class, gender sexuality and ability/disability and thus temporary ambiguities might occur that reposition the subject either on the margins of whiteness, or in a situa-tion where action might be possible. As Leonardo (2009) states, '...whites exist at the intersection of discourses that struggle for supremacy over their subjectivity. They exist in multiple worlds and have had to make decisions about traversing the racial landscape (101). These palimpsests in whiteness (which, as Levine-Rasky [2002] rightly considers is nothing more than a false identity – see also Leonardo 2009), like a television picture suddenly flickering in a storm, conveys to the white person the temporality and insub-stantiality of whiteness even though hegemonic ideologies try to establish the picture as clear, strong and infinite. The various ways in which working class white people (Bonnett 2000; Preston 2010), white immigrants (Roediger 2002, 2005) and white women (Walter 2001) have been posi-tioned on the fringes of white respectability are key examples where, if whiteness itself is not challenged, such groups are given a liminal position-ing within whiteness. In addition, such liminal positionings within whiteness can create the historical circumstances in which alliances between whites and people of colour become possible even to the extent of the rejection of majoritarian whiteness (Ignatiev, 1995). So the contextualisation of white-ness might (according to Levine-Rasky) disrupt white privilege, but it also can disrupt the basis of solidarity on which such privilege is founded.

Secondly, there are the Foucauldian critiques of RT, such as those of Kannen (2008) and McWhorter (2005). These consider the visible privilege of white bodies as preventing individual RT's from stepping outside of whiteness as a category. Kannen considers that in adopting the RT position '...whiteness is challenged, but reinforced as *something*' (Kannen 2008, 154) and that due to embodiment it is not possible to 'destroy, denounce or escape the whiteness that is of one's *choosing*' (Kannen 2008, 155, empha-sis added) and that the 'sovereign subject' of whiteness then chooses to deploy, or resist, whiteness as a locus of choice (McWhorter 2005, 548). This stance ignores considerations of political economy or the 'operation of white subjectivity within whiteness' (551, quoted in Preston 2010). How-ever, although leaving whiteness can be considered a 'choice' so to is remaining within whiteness. Passivity is a political act. In short, 'Nothing is still a programme, even nihilism is a dogma' (Virilio 2000, 61). Even in a liberal framework of property, choices and rights, then, we might consider that whiteness as property (the guarding of whiteness as property) requires daily tacit choices by whites in accepting white privilege. White people occupy a space of personhood in whiteness but their privileges are built on everyday acts of white supremacy. Even in sleep, the world turns and white agents make the most of investments in whiteness, whether it is the guided drones over Pakistan, the white owned capital in Mexican sweatshops, or other whites who support our career, relationship and lifestyle choices. To drop from this personhood requires active resistance, but to remain within it requires active maintenance in the structures of white supremacy. So the 'choice' to support whiteness requires the tacit support (of whites), who unquestioningly accept the benefits of whiteness. This (passive) acceptance of white privilege should also be seen as (active) participation in white violence. As Shannon (2009, 187) identifies, we need to use language which does not privilege '...hegemonic discourses and the passive voice.' For example, the United States does not '...put more prisoners in jail than any other industrialised country' it 'cages more people,' and 'violence against women' is more properly 'men's violence against women.' Similarly, white privilege pulls 'discursive punches' (Shannon 2009) compared to 'white violence against people of colour.' Theories of white supremacy sometimes begin with the principle of unfair exchange which means that in exchanges between R1 (whites) and R2 (people of colour) (in Mills' [2003], terms) the R1s gain at the expense of the R2s. The problem is that this conception of white supremacy (R1 status) degrades into a moral argument about 'fairness' without some sense of violence or coercion. Leonardo (2009) makes an important shift from white privilege to white supremacy, when he makes the statement that rather than white people finding that money is put into their pockets, money is taken from the pockets of people of colour – except that this implies that there is no resistance and that whites are in some way unequivocally able to do this. A more accurate description might be that the money is taken by violent struggle. Naming violence in this way makes white supremacy more a continuum of violence rather than being bifurcated by covert and overt oppressions. This also removes white supremacy from some of the contractual elements contained within it which are problematic as they reduce white supremacy to a contracting problem in the domain of liberal market relations rather than a systemic one bound up with the inhuman domination of capital and white supremacy. The benefits which whites receive through inhabiting whiteness are not a contracting problem (e.g. one in which a reallocation of resources between whites and people of colour would solve white supremacy in perpetuity) but relations based on the continual exercise of power and oppression. The 'choice' by whites to remain a passive recipient of the benefits of white supremacy is *already* a violent one.

In conclusion then, RT is therefore most certainly not about changing an 'embodiment' and leaving whiteness in any physical sense. In a liberal sense there are ways of changing one's apparent phenotype through tanning or skin lightening products, hair dyes, plastic surgery, clothing and 'acting' but, in most cases, these transformations are not indicative of an actual desire to change 'race' in the same way that drag is not normally associated with a desire to change 'gender' (although both may be associated with a disruption to, a reorientation of, in short a queering of categories). On the contrary, RT is not about whites becoming 'not white.' Rather, by confronting the power structures that police whiteness (Bailey 1998), RT should involve confusing and disrupting the circuits of whiteness so that the state and capital cannot *trust* that white people will act in the interests of white supremacy. RT can be thought of as a technology of transgression (Chakrabarty 2011) but not as a bodily technology. A counter-narrative thought experiment will illustrate that changing embodiment does not change whiteness. If white disappeared as a phenotypic category overnight (as in the crass 1970s film *Watermelon Man*), whites would soon find a way to recapture the privileges of 'whiteness.' Terms would proliferate such as 'formally white' or 'blood white' which would soon be reduced down to 'white.' This loss of phenotypical whiteness would be regarded as a tragedy or a disease, even though some whites would relish the chance at boundary crossing, but we suspect that even the boundary crossing whites would want to return to whiteness in the end, taking advantage of its symbolic privileges. The sentimentalising of former whiteness would mean that the boundaries of whiteness would be firmly policed to prevent people of colour entering the 'formally white category. *So the disappearance of whiteness as skin colour even as a totality would not put an end to racial oppression based on racist white supremacy.* The end of 'white' would not be the end of 'whiteness.'

Race Traitor within Critical Race Theory: towards an activist, public pedagogy

We now move on to consider the relevance of RT for an England in which inequalities are growing, and spaces for resistance shrinking, arguing that by drawing on insights from CRT, the notion of RT may be able to allow us to move towards developing a public pedagogy in which firstly, whites play a role in the struggle against racial inequality, and secondly, racial oppression and the abolition of white supremacy is explicitly foregrounded in movements such as Anarchist Federation, London Class War and Antifa, whose politics to date has tended to be deracialised.

Unlike critical pedagogy, public pedagogy is aimed at pedagogical activity in the public sphere: '...spaces, sites, and languages of education and learning that exist outside schools' (Sandlin and Burdick 2010, 349). We would argue that the difference between critical pedagogy and public pedagogy is significant in that, despite its rhetoric concerning praxis, critical pedagogy is still strategically centred on arenas of learning whether the classroom, adult education or informal education. This leads to fundamental problems in praxis. Classroom, or adult education, based critical pedagogy is dependent upon the resources of the state (often seemingly subverted by appropriation), but state resources nevertheless, and a 'critical rationalism' that enables theory to be transferred to the public sphere (Ellsworth 1994). Public pedagogy, as explained, not only examines popular cultural forms as sites of learning but also understands direct political action to be a site of pedagogy and politics. We argue, then, that CRT provides an alternative way to operationalise RT by connecting it to recently emerging strands of public pedagogy. However, to do so, we need to reinterpret RT in the light of recent insights from CRT.

Although Critical Race Theorists are largely sympathetic to the RT position, they provide a useful corrective to the emphasis in RT on white positionality and the consideration that it is possible to form a course of action within a white perspective alone. As discussed above, although Ignatiev and Garvey (1996) considered that African American resistance to racial oppression was at the vanguard of anti-capitalist activity, much of the theorising of the RT position, both in the book and journals, is from whites. A public pedagogy, then, could usefully be informed by the work of critical race theorist Richard Delgado. In *Rodrigo's Eleventh Chronicle* (1997), Delgado considers the drawbacks of false empathy, where whites paternalistically believe that they can have knowledge and guide actions to end racial oppression:

> '...false empathy is worse than none at all, worse than indifference. It makes you over-confident, so that you can easily harm the intended beneficiary. You are apt to be paternalistic, thinking you know what the other really wants or needs, you can easily substitute your own goal for hers. You visualize what you would want if you were she, when your experiences are radically different, and your needs too. You can end up thinking that race is no different from class, that blacks are just whites who happen not to have any money right now' (614)

These charges of 'false empathy' can potentially be levelled at Race Traitor as it adopts a perspective arising from a white position (albeit one formed through participating in revolutionary activity with people of colour) and collapses 'race' into a counter-revolutionary (but potentially anti-capitalist) force rather than possessing autonomy. Despite these reactionary tendencies in RT, though, Delgado sees a role in RT for militant whites in the struggle against racial oppression as does Bell (1992). In a useful corrective to the critiques considered above, which equate RT with a desire to achieve a post-racial state, Delgado considers that the issue is one of how whites might '...identify with blacks radically and completely, not by imagining how they would feel if they were black, but by identifying themselves with blacks when other whites ask for their help in reinforcing white supremacy' (615).

Furthermore, Delgado considers that even without adopting the principles of RT wholeheartedly, whites (particularly in academia) should consider white audiences and activity other than those of other white liberals.

In particular, white activists informed by CRT should shift from being 'Crits in elite positions' to educate citizens in '...the factories and lower-class tenement districts.... Empathy, the shallow, chic kind – is always more attractive than responsibility, which is hard work' (617). This position resonates with RT in terms of direct action and collective activism with working class, white people. However, we would warn against assuming that white 'Crits in elite positions' have necessarily a more developed understanding of racism than the English (or international) working class. Firstly, in terms of CRT in England few CRT academics are 'in elite positions.' Many hail from a working class background and the majority (including the contributors to this volume) work in universities more akin to the US 'community college' model. Secondly, the working class have often been at the vanguard of struggle against racism and intellectuals have often had to keep up and learn from this struggle.

The public pedagogy could also draw on the work of Leonardo (2009), who considers that the RT project directly confronts and questions white attachments to whiteness and addresses the question of white empathy. For Leonardo, the focus of RT on action is historically contextualised by considering the difference between 'white bodies' and 'white persons when they become *articulated* with whiteness' (102). However, if RT is simply concerned with action there is a danger that '...white abolitionists do not have to face up to whiteness, which sounds too familiar' (105). An 'ironic' or 'falsely empathetic' RT stance simply re-inscribes whiteness, so action is important, but so too is awareness. Leonardo also suggests that activist forms of anti-racism, despite not having the abolition of whiteness as a goal, may have similar consequences to the RT position '...dismantling whiteness as racism leads to the eventual breakdown of whiteness as a social category' (100). An example of this would be a conversation one of us, Charlotte (who is so-called white), had with a group of students (who are of African Caribbean origin) she was interviewing about experiences of racism in their school. The discussion took place in the context of Charlotte's PhD study, which explored minority ethnic young people's school experiences and aimed to foreground the voices of the young people themselves in order to investigate in more depth discourses around race and difference and the ways in which students and staff negotiate these. The study took an ethnographic approach and focus groups with young people from Key Stage 4 (aged 15–16) were conducted at five inner-city schools in the north of England. The following extract is taken from the second meeting with this group.

> Jaya: The way she goes on, it's like, my skin colour shows that I'm black, but I won't act like I'm black.
>
> CC: What's acting like you're black?

Sam and Jaya: Just being normal!

CC: Can I not do it?

Sam: Anybody can do it!

CC: So it's not to do with your skin colour?

All: No!

Jaya: Like how you're acting now, Charlotte, yeah, you're acting perfectly normal, like us, that's black!

By taking an anti-racist stance during the discussion, it could be argued that Charlotte had 'troubled – the boundaries of "Whiteness" as a regime of truth; so much so that my credentials as a White person were now in jeopardy. Put simply, the act of challenging white supremacy was calling in to question the possibility of me being white. At this fundamental level, White people embody White Supremacy' (Gillborn 2008, 200). Like Gillborn, in a similar situation, we feel it is important to be aware of the dangers of individual identity politics, and Charlotte takes no 'ironic' pleasure in this incident. However it firmly illustrates how closely racism and white habituation are connected in that anti-racism is considered to be impossible (by some people) from within white embodiment. CRT's emphasis on activism and tacit support for the Race Traitor project is therefore tempered by the perversity of white supremacy where even an active white rejection of whiteness can strengthen it. It therefore provides a useful corrective to the charge that white people can guide a revolutionary struggle against whiteness.

Ahmed (2004) warns that, in making utterances concerning one's whiteness and one's personal racism (and in declaring it that is also declaring one's anti-racism) white speakers 'perform' anti-racism:

'...the task for white subjects would be to stay implicated in what they critique, but in turning towards their role and responsibility in these histories of racism, as histories of this present, to turn away from themselves, and towards others' (Ahmed 2004: http://www.borderlands.net.au/vol3no2_2004/ ahmed_declarations.htm)

Although the performative might still be a strategy against racial oppression (in that sometimes acts, even without full political consciousness, can have positive political consequences), without the critiques from CRT, which remind whites of the centrality of struggle by people of colour, RT would fall into the same traps that Ahmed has discussed above. The performative may even act as a way for whites to adopt a new form of 'activist' racism-as-anti-racism by removing personal responsibility from the self as implicated in racism through its turn towards direct action. However, RT, tempered by the critiques from Critical Race Theory, turns whites away from performative anti-racism and towards (potentially) activist, situationist and anarchist activities.

Using post-colonial theory, Sandlin and Burdick (2010) consider that one of the tasks of public pedagogy is to consider what they call the *pedagogical Other*, that is a pedagogical form that exists outside of our academic understanding of research, scholarship or pedagogy (critical or otherwise). This is not an 'Other' as subject, but an 'Other' as alternative pedagogy which is not dependent on the tropes of formal education. This form can not be 'captured' by the state or by the intellectual elites, as critical pedagogy so easily can. This is a public pedagogy which, informed by both RT and CRT, reigns in some of RT's white-centeredness, foregrounds the activism of people of colour, provides an activist and situationist alternative to the performative for white people, makes explicit the connections between critical race activism, and activism based on Marxist or Anarchist traditions, and aims to bring together intellectuals and activists across lines of class and race. This seems to be at least a starting position for a pedagogical engagement with, and expansion of, the ideas presented in Race Traitor particularly as the 1968 crisis in capitalism and hegemony, through which the STO were formed, seems slight compared with the current historical situation.

References

Acosta, A. 2009. Two undecidable questions in thinking in which anything goes. In *Contemporary anarchist studies: An introductory anthology of anarchy in the academy*, ed. R. Amster, A. DeLeon, L. Fernandez, A. Nocella II, and D. Shannon, 26–34. London: Routledge.

Ahmed, S. 2004. Declarations of whiteness: The non-performativity of anti-racism. *Borderlands e-journal* 3. http://www.borderlands.net.au/vol3no2_2004/ahmed_declarations.htm.

Ayers, W. 2010. Protest, activism, resistance: Public pedagogy and the public square. In *Handbook of public pedagogy*, ed. J. Sandlin, B. Schultz, and J. Burdick, 619–24. London: Routledge.

Bailey, A. 1998. Locating traitorous identities: Toward a view of privilege-cognizant white character. *Hypatia* 13: 27–42.

Bell, D. 1992. *Divining a racial realism theory in Faces at the Bottom of the Well*. New York: Basic Books.

Bey, H. 1991. *T.A.Z.: The Temporary Autonomous Zone, ontological anarchy, poetic terrorism*. Brooklyn, NY: Autonomedia.

Bonnett, A. 2000. How the British working class became white. In *White identities: Historical and international perspectives*, ed. A. Bonnett, 28–45. London: Prentice Hall.

Bruce, T. 2004. *The death of right and wrong: Exposing the Left's assault on our culture and values*. New York: Three Rivers Press.

Chakrabarty, N. 2011. Beyond culture: From Beyoncé's dream, 'if you thought I would wait for you, you got it wrong' (2008), to the age of Michelle Obama. In *Intersectionality and 'race' in education*, ed. K. Bhopal and J. Preston, 178–91. London: Routledge.

Cole, M. 2009a. *Critical race theory and education: A Marxist response*. London: Palgrave.

Cole, M. 2009b. The color line and the class struggle: A Marxist response to critical race theory as it arrives in the UK. *Power and Education* 1, no. 1: 111–24.

Cole, M. 2009c. Critical race theory comes to the UK: A Marxist critique. *Ethnicities* 9, no. 2: 246–69.

Cole, M. 2009d. On 'white supremacy' and caricaturing Marx and Marxism: A response to David Gillborn's 'Who's afraid of critical race theory in education?'. *Journal for Critical Education Policy Studies* 7, no. 1. http://www.jceps.com/PDFs/07-1-02.pdf.

Cole, M., and A. Maisuria. 2007. 'Shut the f*** up', 'You have no rights here': Critical race theory and racialisation in post-7/7 racist Britain. *Journal for Critical Education Policy Studies* 5, no. 1. http://www.jceps.com/?pageID=article&articleID=85.

Davies, C.B. 2002. Against race, or the politics of self ethnography. *Jenda: A Journal of Culture and African Women Studies* 2, no. 1. http://www.africaknowledgeproject.org/index.php/jenda/article/view/74.

Delgado, R. 1997. Rodrigo's eleventh chronicle: Empathy and false empathy. In *Critical white studies: Looking behind the mirror*, ed. R. Delgado and J. Stefancic. Philadelphia: Temple University Press.

Ellsworth, E. 1994. Why doesn't this feel empowering? Working through the repressive myths of critical pedagogy. In *The Education Feminism Reader*, ed. L. Stone and D. Boldt. London: Routledge.

Gillborn, D. 2008. Racism and education: Coincidence or conspiracy. London: Routledge.

Gilroy, P. 2000. Black fascism. *Transition* 9, no. 1–2: 70–91.

Ignatiev, N. 1980. Introduction to the United States: An autonomist political history. STO pamphlet: http://www.sojournertruth.net/.

Ignatiev, N. 1995. *How the Irish became white*. New York: Basic Books.

Ignatiev, N., and J. Garvey. 1996. *Race traitor*. London: Routledge.

Ignatiev, N., S. Lynd, and K. Lawrence. 1975. Fighting racism: An exchange. STO pamphlet: http://www.sojournertruth.net/.

Kannen, V. 2008. Identity treason: Race, disability, queerness, and the ethics of (post)identity practices. *Culture, Identity and Theory* 49, no. 2: 149–63.

Leonardo, Z. 2009. *Race, whiteness and education*. London: Routledge.

Levine-Rasky, C. 2002. Critical/relational/contextual: Towards a model for studying whiteness. In *Working through whiteness: International perspectives*, ed. C. Levine-Rasky. London: SUNY.

Lewiston Evening Journal. Anti-Jewish decrees in Reich are severe: Jewish woman jailed as 'Race Traitor.' First published November 16th, 1935: http://news.google.com/newspapers?id=bfI0AAAAIBAJ&sjid=7WkFAAAAIBAJ&pg=3398,3869797&dq=race-traitor&hl=en.

Lott, E. 1993. *Love and theft: Blackface minstrelsy and the American working class*. New York: Oxford University Press.

Malott, C. 2006. From pirates to punk rockers: Pedagogies of insurrection and revolution: The unity of Utopia. *Journal for Critical Education Policy Studies* 4, no. 2. http://www.jceps.com/print.php?articleID=70.

Matthews, R. 1932. 'Lemus Discusses Tuskagee', originally published in the 'Afro-American.' November 24th, 1934. http://news.google.com/newspapers?id=9xEnAAAAIBAJ&sjid=NwMGAAAAIBAJ&pg=2691,5766865&dq=race-traitor&hl=en.

McWhorter, L. 2005. Where do white people come from? A Foucaultian critique of Whiteness Studies. *Philosophy and Social Criticism* 31, no. 5–6: 533–56.

Mills, C. 2003. *From 'class' to race: Essays in white Marxism and black radicalism*. Lanham, MD: Rowman and Littlefield.

Nomous, A. 2001. Race, anarchy and punk rock: The impact of cultural boundaries within the anarchist movement. Unpublished handout, Bay Area Anarchist Conference. http://www.phillyimc.org/en/node/38152.

Olson, J. 2009. The problem with infoshops and insurrections: US anarchism, movement building and the racial order. In *Contemporary anarchist studies: An introductory anthology of anarchy in the academy*, ed. R. Amster, A. DeLeon, L. Fernandez, A. Nocella II, and D. Shannon, 35–45. London: Routledge.

Preston, J. 2010. Prosthetic white hyper-masculinities and 'disaster education'. *Ethnicities* 10: 331–43.

Roediger, D. 2002. *Coloured white: Transcending the racial past*. Berkeley, CA: University of California Press.

Roediger, D. 2005. *Working towards whiteness: How America's immigrants became white.* Cambridge, MA: Basic Books.

Sandlin, J., and J. Milam. 2010. Culture jamming as critical public pedagogy. In *Handbook of public pedagogy*, ed. J. Sandlin, B. Schultz, and J. Burdick. London: Routledge.

Sandlin, J., and J. Burdick. 2010. Inquiry as answerability: Toward a methodology of discomfort in researching critical public pedagogies. *Qualitative Inquiry* 16, no. 5: 349–60.

Shannon, D. 2009. As beautiful as a brick through a bank window: Anarchism, the academy and resisting domestication. In *Contemporary anarchist studies: An introductory anthology of anarchy in the academy*, ed. R. Amster, A. DeLeon, L. Fernandez, A. Nocella II, and D. Shannon, 183–6. London: Routledge.

Stovall, D. 2010. A note on the politics of place and public pedagogy: Critical race theory, schools, community and social justice. In *Handbook of public pedagogy*, ed. J. Sandlin, B. Schultz, and J. Burdick. London: Routledge.

Virilio, P. 2000. *Strategy of deception.* London: Verso.

Walter, B. 2001. *Outsiders inside: Whiteness, place and Irish Women.* London: Routledge.

Weyl, N. 1979. *Karl Marx, racist.* New Rochelle, NY: Arlington House.

Zack, N. 1999. 'White ideas'. In *Whiteness: Feminist and philosophical reflections*, ed. C. Coumo and K.Q. Hall, 77–84. Lanham, MD: Rowman and Littlefield.

Filmography

Watermelon Man. Directed by Melvin Van Peebles. Los Angeles, CA: Columbia Pictures Corporation, 1970.

What's the point? Anti-racism and students' voices against Islamophobia

Shirin Housee

In a climate of Islamophobic racism, where media racism saturates our TV screens and newspapers, where racism on the streets, on campus, in our community become everyday realities, I ask, what can we – teachers, lecturers and educationalists – do in the work of anti-racism in education? This article examines classroom debates on Islamophobia by exploring the connections between student experiences and the wider social political issues and ideologies that create and re-enforce racism. The underlying interest for me is to examine the ways in which classroom interaction; dialogue and exchanges can undo racist thinking by informed anti-racist critique. This article has three sections; first, I discuss the multicultural and anti-racist discourses within education in the British context. I then go on to explore theoretical developments found in Critical Race Theory (CRT) as a tool for this anti-racism in education. In the second section I examine Islamophobia, the hatred of Muslims, as a measurement of current racism. My interest is to explore the meanings of Islamophobia, and its relevance to students lived realities. Media representation and text on Islamophobia are used as a way of pulling out the student views and lived experiences of such racism. In the final section I raise the question of *'what's the point of studying racism?'* Here I discuss a class seminar on the viewing of a YouTube role play of a racist incident against a hijaab wearing woman. The *point here* is to unpack student's views and reactions to Islamophobia. I conclude that classroom discussions can be a place where anti-racist, anti-sexist and anti-oppressive views emerge to inform the discussion for social justice in education.

Introduction

My awakening to racism and anti-racism begin with a reflection of my own student life and my political awakening that has inspired my interest in anti-racism in education. One day, in January 1981 during my A level studies, my lecturer stormed into class appearing very agitated and upset. He asked: *Does anyone know what happened this weekend*? We looked at each other confused and said no we did not. He then spread out on our desks the weekend papers. *Fire ablaze, fire bombed teenagers party, thirteen dead in house fire, 13 youth died in a racist arson attack.*

This was the first I had heard of the firebomb attack of a black teenager's birthday party, which had taken place on the previous Saturday. New Cross Fire was a devastating house fire, which killed 13 young black teenagers in New Cross, southeast London on Sunday January 18, 1981. I was of a similar age. Immersed in a state of disbelieve, I found myself thinking, this could have been my party, the 13 dead could have been my friends or me. This was a moment of truth. Racism was not just the stuff of books, it was not about the far away and the long ago, it was the here and now, on our streets, and in our homes.

The reading of these headlines and the subsequent articles were frightening to a teenage group studying the politics of race and racism. I remember thinking racism claims lives. I asked myself repeatedly, who were the culprits? And what were the police doing? Questions of right and wrong, and of justice, became commonplace in our classroom thereafter.

The black community suspected that this house fire was an arson attack motivated by racism. The Action Committee accused the London Metropolitan Police of covering up the cause, the protests arising out of the fire led to a mobilisation of black political activity. Nobody has ever been charged in relation to the fire.

Our student group were outraged by this lack of justice. Within weeks our student group developed into an anti-racist activist campaigning group. Our first task was to mobilise for the national demonstration against this racist attack. On Monday March 2 1981, the Action Committee organised the 'Black People's Day of Action.' Our student group joined the march for justice. As we lined up in Hyde Park behind the 13 cardboard coffins symbolising the 13 dead, I remember very harrowingly, the emotions that overwhelmed me that day and the flood of tears that rolled down my face. Over 20,000 people went on this anti-racist march, we marched for eight hours or more, from Fordham Park to Hyde Park, shouting slogans like: *'Thirteen Dead and Nothing Said,' 'No Police Cover-Up,' 'Blood Ah Go Run, if Justice nah Come.'* I was moved and empowered by the activism of my college/friendship group. Anti-racism became real and taking action became a necessity. *This was my political awakening.*

My awakening to the reality of racism and to the importance of anti-racist campaigns has impacted on my very being. This political and personal journey has made me the feminist and anti-racist teacher that I have become. Teaching and learning for me are not processes that can be detached from the real world. My practice in class, that is, my pedagogy, and the curriculum, is constantly reviewed by questions of social justice. My role as a teacher cannot be divorced from the social world that we belong to. Fundamentally, I cannot view my teaching as simply 'academic.' Knowing about oppression triggers an emotion to 'drive out,' or 'should out' against such injustice around us. This passion has been the drive behind my activism and my teaching practise.

This article shares a couple of teaching sessions on anti-Muslim racism and media issues as examples of how I do anti-racism in my class at present.

From multicultural education, anti-racist education – to Critical Race Theory

Before I turn to the current debates on anti-racist education and Islamophobia, I first reflect on the 1970's and 1980's multicultural debate in education as experienced in the British context. Britain is a socially and culturally plural society. Education policies have tried to reflect these changes. The 1970's multicultural debate in education spoke of co-existence, integration, tolerance and diversity. Whilst these policy changes were important for its time, within a decade, these multicultural policies were soon accused of tokenism. The policies did not link the failures, exclusions and alienation of ethnic minority children in education with the overall structures of racism, within which schools function, but instead, as said by Solomos (Cashmore and Bains 1988, 171).

> Multicultural education was a reflection of the common-sense and policy notion that black pupils are the target group which policies should aim at since it is their (blackness) 'deficiencies and 'problems' that have to be overcome. Even when clothed in progressive language, this view tends to support the notion that it is West Indians or Asian children that cause problems for schools and not vice-versa.

Such critiques of multicultural education paved the way to the anti-racist movement in education. Educational inequality of ethnic minorities was squarely placed within the wider socio-economic inequalities that disproportionately failed and excluded Black and ethnic minority children in education. In going beyond the educational system, the anti-racist critique argued that structural and societal inequalities and institutional racism was key to the understanding of ethnic minority educational inequalities. (Gillborn 1995; Troyna and Carrington 1990; Figueroa 1999; Cashmore and Bains 1988; Troyna 1987; Mac An Ghail 1988. These developments have been important, but as Gillborn (2006a) argues, there is still a long way to go before anti-racist endeavours comply with the basics of the new race equality legislation (Race Relations Amendment Act 2002). He goes on to say: 'anti-racism has not failed – in most cases, it simply has not been tried yet' (2006a, 17) he continues by suggesting that:

a radical perspective is required to cut through the superficial rhetorical changes and address the more deep-rooted state of race inequality in the education system.

In my attempt to get to the deep-root of racism in education, I turn to critical race theory (CRT). CRT has its roots in US legal scholarship, Bell (1992), Crenshaw et al. (1995), Delgado (1995), and Williams (1993), are often referred to as the founders of this movement. In the last decade CRT has crossed over to other disciplines including Sociology, History, Women's Studies and Education. And through the work of Gillborn (2006a, 2006b, 2008) it has now arrived to Britain. CRT has no single statement of what it is, rather, as Gillborn suggests, CRT is a perspective that is growing, adapting and adopting new ideas. And as a perspective 'it is a set of interrelated beliefs about the significance of race and racism, and how it works in western societies." (Gillborn 2006a, 19). To this end, CRT has a series of defining elements and conceptual tools. Firstly, it argues that racism is endemic and is deeply ingrained legally and culturally in Society. Secondly, the concept objectivity is false because there is no neutrality and third, experiential knowledge of people of colour should be welcomed via a 'call for context' (Delgado 1995). Finally, and most importantly to this article, CRT links anti-racism to social justice issues. CRT is constantly developing and evolving through a continued reciprocal dialogue between scholarship and activism. Ladson-Billings and Tate (2006) were the first to apply CRT to education. They claim that the continued racial discrimination in schools and colleges, the race specific pedagogic issues of curricular and the marginalisation of black students in classroom teaching, continue to be features of the education institution in the United States. In this critique they highlight the importance of black cultural identities in its analysis of such issues. Confirming this view, Solórzano and Yosso (2009, 132) argues that:

> Critical race theory... in education...works toward the elimination of racism... [It] is a set of insights, perspectives, methods, and pedagogy that seeks to identify, analyze and transform the structural and cultural aspects of education that maintain subordination and dominant racial narratives in and out of the classroom.

CRT in education examines not only the macro picture of policies, strategies, programmes, and related practice across the entire educational endeavour, but also focuses on the micro picture of interpersonal behaviour, classroom interaction, participation, and related matters. One of the most relevant conceptual *tools* for my work is that of counter-narratives. CRT scholars have established the use of story telling as central to connecting the voice of the victims of racism with the documenting of institutional, overt and covert racism. For CRT the use of narrative or voice is central to the making of knowledge. This is a controversial point – because CRT values marginal voices and sees experiential knowledge as legitimate knowledge. Although CRT holds a firm stance against notions of racial essentialism, CRT contends that the social realities of minorities give them experiences, voices, and viewpoints that are likely to be different from mainstream dominant narratives. This is where counter-voice or in Baszile's (2008, 263) word *testimonies* – become imperative:

> Our testimonies are an opportunity to ponder the connections between our individual experiences of race...to understand how race and racism drive different interpretations of reality...critical race testimony is a form of pedagogical protest as it works to disrupt our understanding...it seeks to bear out a fuller report of racism.

The work of anti-racism from a CRT perspective requires that educators not only make use of material and content that challenges racism, but also connects these materials with student narratives and experiences, as Fishman and McCarthy (2005, 349) say here:

> Multicultural texts and students narratives need to be contextualised if they are to be instructive...(in a way) that helps students place their stories in broader historical, and/or philosophic contexts so they can forge connections between their views and of larger themes.

Part of the CRT thesis of connecting the smaller world of classroom discussions to the bigger socio-economic and political world, is to engage with social justice issues and to make a commitment to change in society. CRT's theoretical developments have provided me with a more radical critique of racism in education. CRT is both an academic discipline that theoretically analyses race and racism, and is also a tool that can be used in the practise of resistance – praxis. In this sense CRT has, in my view, revitalized critical anti-racism in a way that offers a coherent and challenging set of insights and conceptual tools that provides, as Gillborn (2006b, 258) claims here, an:

> ...understanding of how antiracists and critical race theorists have approached certain issues and dilemmas. Both share a concern not merely to document but to change; they are engaged in praxis.

It is within the social justice debate in education, that this article explores issues of Islamophobia and anti-racism in an educational context: In the final section of this article, I return to CRT's discussion of anti-racism and social justice issues. First, I explore media racism with specific reference to Islamophobia. Part of my endeavour here is to explore student observations as they critique the raced and gendered specific Islamophobic messages in the mainstream media.

Islamophobia – *new right* racism in the media – how *I teach against it*

Britain is a multicultural society with people from many countries and from many religious backgrounds. This new reality calls for new analysis. Today's context requires that we consider the 'new' racisms of our time. One such reality is Islamophobia (Conway 1997) – the hatred of Muslim people and their religion – Islam. Although Islamophobia is a relatively new term, anti-Muslim racism has, however, existed for centuries. It is, as Said (1981) reminds us, based on a very old prejudice. It is a racism that is justified by cultural and religious difference, hence – unemployment, discrimination, poverty, marginalisation and indeed, criminalization of Muslims, are now viewed through 'cultural lens.' Stolcke (cited in Fekete 2006) has referred to this as cultural fundamentalism. Islamophobia, he argues, is a form of racism that excludes and marginalises populations *not* on the basis of their biological difference but on their 'so-called' incommensurable cultural differences. This is a closed view of Islam, which prevails in popular discourses on Muslims. Islam has and continues to be portrayed as inferior, primitive, violent, irrational, oppressive and undemocratic. This is juxtaposed with the West as civilized, reasonable, sophisticated, enlightened, and democratic (Conway 1997).

The media plays a fundamental role in the construction of knowledge and are a key source through which identities in relation to the 'Other' is constructed (Van Dijk 1993, 243). The events of 9/11 and 7/7, together with the invasion of Iraq, Afghanistan and the 'war on terror,' have been used to bring Muslims/Muslim identity to the forefront of global media. Since then an increasingly intense focus has been placed on the world's Muslim population, and particularly those Muslims living in the West. Muslim women wearing the hijaab, and men with beards, or any other dress code associated with Islam, has provoked hostility. In Britain, the 7th July 2005 London bombings and the realisation that these acts were carried out by Muslims born and raised in the country, has led to increased anxiety concerning British Muslim youth (Abbas 2007, 8). In its scaremongering tactics, the press, for example, has succeeded in creating a moral panic concerning an internal terrorist threat constructed around a new *folk devil* – that of the young British Muslim male (Abbas 2001,248). Asian male masculinities are read through images of 'terrorist youth' juxtaposed with the passivity of 'Asian Muslim female femininities.'

Media discourse is one of the primary arenas in which the debate concerning the discourse of 'the Muslims'/and Islam has been played out. The literature regarding media representations of Islam and Muslims generally cohere in their identification of a pattern of negative stereotyping, bias and underlying Islamophobia (Poole 2002). Poole argues that the dominant discourse on Muslims suggest that, '…Muslims are associated with militancy, danger and anti-Western sentiment' (Poole 2002, 42). Said maintains that the media fails to provide a fair representation of Islam and its followers through a mixture of 'ignorance, cultural hostility and racial hatred...' (Poole 2002, 42). Indeed Said (1981, 43) acknowledges this fact when he points out that... 'it is the media that form the "cultural apparatus" through which Europeans and Americans derive their consciousness of Islam.'

In the following part of the article I explore representations of Muslims in the press as a way of drawing out the racism in a teaching class on Islamophobia. Fundamental to this endeavour is to explore teaching methods and material/content that challenges racism. Students' participation in this learning is vital to my project against racism.

Reading Islamophobia: what the class of 2009–10 said

In this part of the article I refer to a discussion by my second level Sociology degree students studying race and racism in the British context. The module examines the theoretical explanations of race and racism, the history of racism and the sociological studies of the different forms of racial discrimination. In the seventh week of the module, the class examined the racism and the racialisation process in the mass media. This seminar session explored the different forms of media racism and then followed through a study of anti-Muslim racism. The class discussed the relevant media texts, particularly exploring the racist representation of minorities in the British context. The class unpacked media messages and made links with the socio-political impacts of these messages. Here students drew on their own lived experiences as they made sense of media racism. A discussion of the misrepresentation of the *other* was particularly useful in understanding the West/ East/Us/other discourse.

In the second seminar session, the class examined a short (five minute) YouTube role play on Islamophobic racism on the street. Students were then asked to reflect on the clip and draw on their wider knowledge and experience of such racism.

I have been teaching race and racism as part of our sociology course at the university for over 20 years now; I have witnessed the changing face of racism and the student response to these changes. My teaching has reflected these changes (Housee 2010). In the 1990s anti-black racism was the most dominant form of racism and the most topical theme for discussion in class. In the new millennium, as our reality and the global socio-economic and political circumstances have changed, so have my teaching and learning references and materials. My current classroom debates often take me to these specific religious, cultural, as well as, racial references and experiences that are now displayed in the media.

With specific reference to Islamophobia we explored the messages and images of Muslims in the British press. We discussed headlines from local and national papers; we examined the use of loaded words and stereotypical images of Muslims during the aftermath of 7th of July 2005 suicide bombings.

One particular theme that dominated class discussion was how the media represented religiosity and masculinity and femininity. A common theme that came through from these students was the media representation of the 'Muslim other' as people who either posed a threat to the nation – the terrorists, with a binary representation that portrays Muslims as law abiding citizens, – for example, the passive female woman. Central to both of these images were notions of loyalty or disloyalty to the nation, such references (as seen below) are often articulated within identity issues of Britishness and otherness.

Methodological issues and findings

A front page image from *The Times* (7th July 2006) of a Muslim male 'terrorist' – Tanweer dressed with an Arab headscarf with the quotation 'what you have witnessed is only the beginning of a string of attacks.' This image was juxtaposed with the image of one of the victims Shahara, here the text said: 'She loved London, she loved Britain... Shahara loved her religion.' This image was projected on the white board. I chose this image because of the seminar discussions around masculinity, femininity, Britishness and nationalism that were reoccurring in the class discussions on Islamophobia. Classes are typically structured with an hour of interactive lecture time, followed by seminar discussion and group activities. The lectures pointed to the sociological studies on Islamophobia in the media (Hafez 2000; Poole 2000, 2002) the students were asked to read this literature ahead of the seminar discussions. The seminars are flexible and unstructured, with students working in discussion groups. The class worked in groups of four to five and studied the image, the story and the headline references.

I circulated between groups; observed and listened, I did not comment or participated but made mental notes, which I then wrote up when I returned to my desk. This session lasted around 15 minutes. At the end of the 15 minutes of seminar discussion, students were asked to write up their comments on shared sheets. A student nominee from each seminar group fed back to the larger class. As the students shared their feedback, the class were invited to intervene by asking questions and to make comments.

At the end of this session the seminar presentation groups were invited to leave their sheets for me to observe. This is voluntary; students are told that the commentaries are used for evaluation and research purposes. This is something I do often. It is my way of reflecting on the class issues and observations. This, for me, is about recognising and indeed recording student voice from my teaching. Sometimes these notes are used in proceeding weeks and are used to develop my teaching generally. Collecting and taking notes, from student discussions, forms part of my teaching journal. This journal is central to my personal reflective observations. I like to keep in check the issues as they arise in class, and to consider the significance of these issues in my own research endeavours.

The following are the notes from the collected sheets from this first seminar session. I have categorised the notes under themes that emerged from the discussion. The first set of notes refers to identity issues, here gendered issues of masculinity and femininity tied to notions of Britishness and belonging were transparent in the students' comments, as seen here:

- This image suggests two binary positions – the right kind of Muslim, innocent, a sweet little girl, compared to the wrong kind of Muslim – a terrorist.
- Muslim identity here is questioned. . .seen as either part of Britain or against Britain – the 'enemy within'. . .either against us or with us, this image is about whether you fit in, or not, in England.

Identity issues, as mentioned above, have been important to my students. What was revealing during the above seminar discussion is the way the students linked the gendered relevance of the image to the scaremongering stereotypes that is imbedded within these images. The students were confident about making the link between the negative portrayals of Muslims and the current political situation. I was therefore, not surprised, that they were able to speak of binary opposites of Muslim male terrorist – the *enemy within*, which was then juxtaposed with the passivity of Asian females, as suggested here:

- The image depicts violence through the racialisation of young Muslim terrorist.
- The media always focuses on Muslim men. . .for suspected terror plots and things. . .but they never show Muslim women. . .when they do, it's about how they're oppressed by the veil. . .
- The media talks about radicalization among British Muslim male youth and how this makes them more susceptible to extremist influences. . .
- I think people aren't worried about Muslim women being radicalised because they think of them as weak rather than aggressive. . .

The second theme from the student comments speaks to the importance of studying media racism. The students here are clear about the role of the media, Islam as they argue, is viewed through the media lens, and because of this, the media is seen to be a vitally important institution, as said here:

- Studying race and racism in the media has given me an idea of how the media works and how people in society get their racist views.
- I was not aware that Islamophobia was a form of racism, but by studying media messages and images it makes sense now.
- Many non-Muslims are not educated on Islam; they are dependent on media portrayal of Muslims. . .. People have negative views, which they have picked up from the media about extremism.

In the following comments students make specific reference to anti-Muslim stereotypes. Specifically these students begin to draw attention to the 'scare-mongering' and the 'folk-devil' creation of Muslims and Muslim men during the 9/11 and 7/7 attacks, as expressed here:

- It is important to understand Muslims and not to make stereotyped opinions (of them)...media stirs up fear, this has an effect on how Muslim men are perceived by the wider British public.
- The irrational fear of Islam and Muslim people has been caused by the recent terror attack and the way the news has portrayed Muslims in the media.
- I believe 9/11 and the 7/7 bombings in London made people resentful about all Muslims...
- 9/11...attack was far away in America, whereas 7/7 has scared people here (UK), young British Muslims are seen to pose a real threat to national security.

The above comments are important, as a teacher I like to believe that students leave class with doing more than observing images. I want to see students make the relevant connections between socio-political issues and the racialised images observed. I want to hear students ask those relevant questions of the role of racism in the media. This class, as seen in the above and indeed in the quotations below, did begin to ask those deeper political questions. The following comments are telling of how students are able to connect media politics and party Politics:

- Islamophobic racism is something that is promoted by politicians; they use the media to portray Muslims in a bad light...
- The media has fuelled fear in us, so the state can justify war on terror/terrorists and take away our civil liberties by introducing identity cards...

Gender issues surrounding Islamophobia have been very vocal in my classes since July 2005. Muslim male students have often shared their experiences of personal harassment. At the end of this class, a Muslim male student approached me and began to speak about his experiences of harassment. I told him that his experiences were very important and needed to be noted. I invited him to write them down and send it to me via e-mail. A week later I received a two-page e-mail response. Here I provide an extensive piece from his written narrative. This is what he wrote.

I think things have definitely got harder for us in Britain post 7/7, especially for Muslim men...the media focus on us as kind of the 'enemy within,'...7/7 I think has scared people, they think maybe young British Muslims could pose a real threat to national security. I certainly think there's an increase in

Islamophobia since the London bombings, but I don't think this is felt in everyday interactions with people, I think it's more so in the media. Personally I don't think radicalization among the youth is anywhere near as bad as they make out. Sure, there may be a small minority of people who have extremist views…this is just a minority. The problem is that the media tends to conflate increased religiosity among us youths as a sign of extremism but that's not the case. I experience the repercussions of 7/7…they target young Asian men more because of these anti-terror laws…. I've been stopped for no reason, and my car has been searched and even though they didn't find anything, the police were still really rude to me, swearing at me and things and I think it's cos they just assume I'm hiding something.

The above quotation, and the prior quotations drawn from the seminar session in class, is very important to this article. Student views and experiences of Islamophobia have thrown light on our teaching in a way that no textbook could reach. Although the last quotation came to me via e-mail and was not shared in class, it is a very important contribution to this discussion. The students of 2009–10 may not have heard this, but the writing on this paper has now made his comments public and for all to read. This was an important seminar; it revealed some of the student views that often do not get shared in wider class discussions. Student voice here is testimony of the richness and the depth of knowledge and understanding that students bring to class. Student's lived experiences, as revealed in the above, are important contributions to the work of anti-racism. Student counter-voice forms the challenge to mainstream perspectives. The student voice, indeed, counter voice, is central to my work of anti-racism in Higher Education.

What is the point? 'Now you know about racism, what ya gonna to do about it?'

In the following section I discuss the second seminar on Islamophobia. Here I follow the theme beyond media racism, I further explore students lived experience of racism, as shared in the last quotation above. My *point* here is to examine the social justice debates within anti-racist education. I was particularly interested to explore whether the experience of racism, could lead to anti-racism and indeed to a personal political transformation of activism, as demonstrated in my own narrative at the beginning of this article. If we agree with Solórzano and Yosso (2009, 133) that, a commitment to social justice must offer a 'transformative response to racial, gender and class oppression that is about elimination of racism, sexism, and poverty and the empowering of subordinated minority groups.' Than, I would argue, we have no choice but to raise the bar, so that anti-racist and anti-oppressive pedagogy is central to our teaching.

For me, the study of racism is rooted in my pedagogical desire that students learn and transform to become critical pedagogues and activists against racism. In the following I explore this further with reference to my own teaching of Islamophobia – anti-Muslim racism.

Teaching in an anti-racist way, is, in my view, a political project. If we argue that the unequal structures, institutions and ideas of racism, and sexism and other oppressive ideologies, are articulated within society and has damaged our understanding and reasoning, then a job (in my view) for the anti-racist 'educator' must be to facilitate the process that help undo oppressive ideas, in order that we can reconstruct progressive ones. My challenge, therefore, is to nurture democratic sentiments that critique discrimination and injustices through teaching that, as Nagda (2003, 168) says: '...fosters a critical consciousness by which students and teachers see their experiences situated in historical, cultural contexts and recognised possibilities for changing oppressive structures.'

Social justice in education takes a moral position that critiques society as unjust towards the marginalised and the excluded. In terms of anti-racism, the focus of this position is twofold: to highlight the moral imperative that racism is wrong, and that the commitment to anti-racist education, is to work to empower learners so they can raise their voice against such racism.

Education for social justice then, takes an approach to learning and teaching based on human rights, active participation, the evaluation of change and the empowerment of people to become actively involved in their own future. Translated into anti-racist/oppressive education practice, this is, according to Clarke and Drudy (2007, 13) about:

> ...reflective practice that requires a conscious, systematic, deliberate process of framing and re-framing classroom practice in light of... democratic principles, educational beliefs, values and the preferred visions which teachers bring to the teaching-learning event.

In my teaching I re-frame class room practice by creating inclusive and interactive teaching spaces. Student's contributions are welcomed and encouraged. I rely on student's discussions by drawing on their lived experiences. This is not just about 'livening' the seminar discussions, it is fundamentally about making lived experiences and the student voices as legitimate sources of knowledge.

I teach modules that explore gender/sexism and race/racism; the literature I offer, invites us to critically think of such oppression and discrimination in our communities. It is therefore inevitable that my teaching asks social justice questions of these issues. My progressive political leanings and my identity as a black Asian woman have helped me utilise my anti-racist and anti-sexist views. Teaching for me, is not neutral, we all have our biases, and the point is to be open about these and to offer other perspectives that allow students to make up their own minds. Without apology, I am transparent about certain views on racism and sexism. Although this is a moral and ethical challenge for me, I do think that if some views are oppressive and wrong, it becomes my desire, that my students should also believe they are wrong (of course some students don't agree with me, and that too is ok), my cards on the table, I agree with McKinny (2005, 389) that my task in the classroom is not 'merely instructive' but one that creates:

> ...a shift in perspective...based on particular values...anti-racism and anti-sexism...under these circumstance then, I cannot pretend that I have no desire to encourage my own goals in the classroom.

In the following, I explore student's views on issues of anti-Muslim racism as social justice issues. In this part of the article I ask, can the study of racism also raise social justice issues? And as my narrative in the introduction suggests, should the study of racism also begin to raise the potential for anti-racist activism? In this final section of the article I explore this point.

From theory to practice – the praxis of anti-racism

Having spent seven weeks discussing race and racism I was now ready to discuss the politics of anti-racism and social justice. In this eighth week of seminar I decided to show a YouTube clip on Islamophobia. The students in class were made aware that this was a fabricated role play incident that was secretly filmed. This film clip is a five-minute role play of a Muslim woman being harassed in a shopping mall. There are three female actors, two actors racially abusing the women with a hijaab and an actor who plays the 'Muslim women' in a hijaab. The passers-by in the shopping mall are not aware that this was a role-play; as far as they were concerned this incident was a real incident. The YouTube clip begins with the narrator asking this question: *Does wearing a headscarf affect how most people perceive Muslim women? And are they less likely to intervene to help a woman in distress who's wearing a headscarf?* The narrator continues by saying *failing to intervene does not break the law* – but asks, *is it morally wrong to do nothing* (http://www.youtube.com/watch?v=RhIwLgNsfwI).

The following is an extract from the transcript of the role-play, which begins with the two female abusers making derogatory references to the woman with a headscarf:

The abusers

> 'Hey what's that on your head? A tea cloth...nice tea towel, top fashion or what – what she got to hide...'

This is repeated until a first white **female** passer by steps in and says:

'Leave her alone'. . .and physically moves the Muslim woman, whilst shouting at the racists to leave.

When interviewed by the cameraman, this **woman** says:

'it was wicked, she looked so vulnerable. It wasn't 'cos she's black, or Indian, it was about the way she was dressed I could not just walk by. . .'

The racist taunting continues with the following:

The abusers

'Do you fancy a bacon sandwich, hey Salman Rushdie's *Satanic Verses*, that was poetry in motion. . .that was. . .bloody terrorists. . .look at the way she's dressed. Looks like a bin liner. . .. It's our country.'

A white male passed by and looks on and smiles. This was his response to the camera interview:

'If I see someone being harassed it's none of my business – I think the British public are the sort of people who stand back and accept things as they are, I would step in if it got violent. . .'

Another white male passer by said to the cameramen:

'should they be allowed to be here? and paused. . .em I don't know'. . .he sniggered.

A second white female passer by intervenes: She pulls the hijaab woman away and confronts the racists. When interviewed and asked why she did so, she said:

'When people abuse somebody because they are different, it's wrong.... I intervened because I think if you can speak up for other people who are experiencing that kind of harassment it's important.'

A white male passer by intervenes and tells the abusers to stop. The role play ends here.

At the end of the role play **the actors** were asked how they felt about doing the role-play. Here are their comments:

We worked very hard at provoking attention; people should have given more attention to the abuse. The first lady was very upset this was re-assuring. It felt good that people are prepared to not stand there and listen to this abuse.

I have watched this video clip many times now. I have led anti-racist discussions at conferences and seminar presentations on the back of this clip. It continues to be a very painful clip for me to watch. It was only after presenting this clip to colleagues, that I found the courage to show it to my students. I was troubled by the concern that some students may have found this clip too voyeuristic and too painful to watch. Given that some of the students had shared their experiences of racial harassment, I was mindful of the emotional difficulty of watching this clip. I told the students about the clip and why I thought it was important to watch. Despite my reservations, I believe as Wagner (2005, 263) says below, that the risk of unsettling the students is worthwhile in the work of anti-racism:

> anti racist pedagogy represents a shift from traditional university teaching practices and as such involves a changed of thinking that will necessarily be unsettling for some students, as it requires them to move beyond their comfortable, deep rooted views of the world.

I chose this video because I wanted to share the reality of everyday racism, and more importantly, I wanted the students to understand that racism is a shared problem and therefore, a shared responsibility. I recognised that this clip would be unsettling, but balanced this, with the bigger social justice issue of anti-racism.

At the end of the viewing there was a deadly silence. I interrupted the silence by suggesting that students' work in groups, but the continued silence convinced me that we should take a short break. As I watched most of the students leave, I began to question whether I had done the right thing in showing the clip; I questioned whether it was too risky, too voyeuristic, and too painful for teaching purposes? Although most students left class, a few remained behind. I approached them and asked how they felt about the video. They assured me that despite it being difficult to watch, they thought it was important for students to see such overt racism, as it made the study of racism real. When the rest of the class returned from their break, I again invited students to reflect on the clip. This time, I asked them to reflect and make individual comments. I then invited students,' if they so wish to share these comments. Some did, but most did not. At the end of the class I invited students to leave their reflective pieces for me to consider.

This practice of inviting students to leave notes is something I do as part of my reflective evaluation, particularly when students do not respond to group work and class discussion. Individual student's comments in this situation become crucial in this reflective work. These student notes form the student voice for my teaching evaluation, general course development and for research purposes. The students are made aware of this and notes are always anonymous.

Using the video clip to raise awareness, reaction and action against Islamophobia was for me about checking to see how students felt about such public racism and what they felt they could and should do in the work against such racism. I asked the students to spend five minutes reflecting on the video clip and asked them to describe how they felt about such overt public racism. The following are a selection of the student's initial thoughts, what is interesting here is that these students were surprised that such racism *still* exists, as said here:

- I was outraged that a country that advocates religious freedom that this woman should go through this.
- I was shocked to see some passer-bys seemed to enjoy such racist taunting.
- I was shocked to see that so many people ignored the abuse.
- The clip was very shocking and upsetting, it was awful to witness such racism. Racism still exists and many people just don't care about it.

The following quotations talk specifically to 'being different' and to be targeted by racist because of this difference, as seen here:

- It should not matter what you look like, where you come from. One should be able to walk down the street without abuse.
- It is sad, we are all different and it is wrong that some people are targeted for being different by racists.

The following speak to the victimisation of Muslims, the first from a non-Muslim perspective and the second student shares how vulnerable she as an Asian feels by a lack of support in Society:

- I feel very bad for hijaab wearing women that go through such racist taunting,
- I left the room feeling vulnerable, and it reminded me that when we Asians are 'out there' we are all alone and there are very few strangers/people who will come to our rescue.

As a teacher who wants to raise the emotionally uncomfortable issue of racism in class, I am always looking for reassurance from students. The quotation below confirms that the video clip and general teaching about Islamophobia is an important endeavour.

- The topic of Islamophobia – anti-Muslim racism...should be discussed within the classroom. So it can be reversed.
- It is important for students to know of the horrors of racism, it is real, racism is everywhere, it shouldn't happen, but it does...

- Ignorance is the main problem; I think that the issue of racism needs to be constantly discussed if we are to be able to make any changes...

Given that one of my objectives of teaching about racism is to raise the critique against it and to welcome activism that just might challenge such racism. Given this, I was warmed by the following comments that allude to taking action against racism.

- I believe that when people witness racism or discrimination taking place within society, people should intervene and tell them it is not right.
- When people witness racism, they should take a stand and tell others, that it is wrong.
- Not enough is done to challenge racism against Muslims.
- This racism should not happen, I like to think that campaigns and legislation will end this...

It is also important to me that students are disheartened by a lack of action against racism, hence these student comments on a lack of intervention is interesting:

- I was deeply disturbed by the inaction of the passer bys; this high-lighted for me the fact that racism is still rife.
- I was not completely surprised by the reactions, as one man in the video said 'Britain is a tolerant society' everyone has a right to their views, I would intervene if it was physical.
- I understand why people don't intervene, because they're worried of what could happen to them. Even I would have to think twice before stepping in.

As I write this article and reflect on the seminar, I again ask, was there any *point* in showing this clip? The best answer I can give to this question is this quote by a Muslim student:

Being a Muslim I have experienced this kind of racist taunting, first hand, and I think it is good that the lecturer raises these issues so other non-Muslims know what we Muslims go through.

The above quotation has reassured and confirmed my view, that the *point* of studying racism, is to be aware of the reality of such racism, and that such awareness may lead to the possibility of anti-racism. I end this section with a reminder from one of the students:

Racism should be challenged. When people witness racism or discrimination taking place, they should take a stand and tell others, that it is wrong.

Where do we go from here? Some concluding thoughts...

Having reflected on the two seminar sessions on Islamophobia and the student comments, I am convinced that the work of anti-racism in university classrooms is fundamentally important. As one student said racism is *real*. Through racism people suffer physically, psychologically, socially, educationally and politically. Our work in university classrooms is just the beginning of this challenge against racisms and other oppressions. Classroom discussions and general teaching form a very important contribution to this work of anti racism in education. There are no short cuts or painless cuts; the work of anti-racism is a difficult one. As educators we should make use of classroom exchanges; students' engaged learning could be the key to promoting anti-racism in our class. My goal is to teach in a way that engages students and leads them to reflect on the socio-economic political/religions issues that surrounds theirs (our) lives.

This article argues for making anti-racist thinking possible in class. The student voice, that critiques mainstream thinking as found in the media and elsewhere, is a starting point for this political work. I argue that teaching and learning in our classroom should encourage the critical consciousness necessary for pursuing social justice. Whilst I acknowledge the limits of doing anti-racist campaign in university spaces, I argue that this is a good starting point. And who knows, these educational exchanges may become (as with my own story) the awakening for bigger political projects against injustices in our society. In conclusion I endorse social justice advocates, such as Cunningham (cited in Johnson-Bailey 2002, 43) who suggest that educators re-direct classroom practices and the curriculum, because: 'if we are not working for equity in our teaching and learning environments, then...educators are inadvertently maintaining the status quo.'

In conclusion I argue that a classroom where critical race exchanges and dialogues take place is a classroom where students and teachers can be transformed. Transformative social justice education calls on people to develop social, political and personal awareness of the damages of racism and other oppressions. I end by suggesting that in the current times of Islamophobic racism, when racist attacks are a daily occurrence, in August and September 2010 alone, nearly 30 people have been racially abused and physically attacked (Institute of Race Relations 2010). The *point of* studying racism, therefore, is to rise to the anti-racist challenge, and for me, a place to start this campaign is within Higher Education Institutions, optimistic as it might sound, I believe, as asserted by Sheridan (cited in Van Driel 2004) that:

'Education can enlighten students and promote positive attitudes.... Education settings can be the first arena in which battles can be fought against Islamophobia. It is to education that our attention should be directed.' (162)

Acknowledgment

I would like to thank Joyce Canaan for her reading of this paper. Her feminist, anti-racist and critical pedagogy has brought much clarity to my writing.

References

Abbas, T., ed. 2001. *Muslim Britain: Communities under pressure*. London: Zed Books.

Abbas, T. 2007. Islamic political radicalism in Western Europe. In *Islamic political radicalism: A European perspective*, ed. T. Abbas, 3–14. Edinburgh: Edinburgh University Press.

Baszile, D.T. 2008. Beyond all reason indeed: The pedagogical promise of critical race testimony. *Race Ethnicity and Education* 11, no. 3: 251–65.

Bell, D. 1992. *Faces at the bottom of the well: The permanence of racism*. New York: Basic Books.

Cashmore, E., and H. Bains. 1988. *Multi-racist Britain*. London: Macmillan.

Clarke, M., and S. Drudy. 2007. Social justice in initial teacher education: Student teachers' reflections on praxis. In *Social justice and intercultural education: An open-ended dialogue*, ed. G. Bhatti, C. Gaine, F. Gobbo, and Y. Leeman, 3–16. Stoke on Trent: Trentham Books.

Conway, G. 1997. Runnymede Trust report. *Islamophobia: A challenge for us all*. London: Runnymede Trust.

Crenshaw, K.W., N. Gotanda, G. Peller, and K. Thomas, eds. 1995. *Critical race theory: Critical writings that formed the movement*. New York: New York Press.

Delgado, R. 1995. *Critical race theory. The cutting edge*. Philadelphia, PA: Temple University Press.

Fekete, L. 2006. Enlightened fundamentalism? Immigration, feminism and the Right. *Race and Class* 48, no. 2: 1–22.

Figueroa, P. 1999. Multiculturalism and anti-racism in a new ERA: A critical review. *Race Ethnicity and Education* 2, no. 2: 281–302.

Fishman, M.S., and L. McCarthy. 2005. Talk about race. When student stories and multicultural curricular are not enough. *Race Ethnicity and Education* 8, no. 4: 347–64.

Gillborn, D. 1995. *Racism and anti-racism in real schools theory, policy, practice*. Buckingham: Open University Press.

Gillborn, D. 2006a. Critical race theory and education: Racism and anti-racism in educational theory and praxis. *Discourse: Studies in the Cultural Politics of Education* 27, no. 1: 11–32.

Gillborn, D. 2006b. Critical race theory beyond North America: Towards a transatlantic dialogue on racism and anti-racism in educational theory and Praxis. In *Critical race theory in education: All God's children got a song*, ed. A.D Dixson and C.K Rousseau, 241–65. New York: Routledge.

Gillborn, D. 2008. *Racism and education. Coincidence or conspiracy*. London: Routledge.

Housee, S. 2010. 'To veil or not to veil': Students speak out against Islam(ophobia) in class. *Enhancing Learning in the Social Sciences (ELiSS)* 2, no.3: http://www.eliss.org.uk/PreviousIssues/Volume2Issue3/AcademicPapers/tabid/291/Default.aspx.

Institute of Race Relations. 2010. http://www.irr.org.uk/2010/september/ms000025.html. http://www.youtube.com/watch?v=RhIwLgNsfwI) Islamophobia Test Islam People reaction to woman in Hijab).

Johnson-Bailey, J. 2002. Race matters: The unspoken variable in the teaching-learning transaction. *New Directions for Adult and Continuing Education* 93: 39–49.

Ladson-Billings, G., and F.W. Tate. 2006. Towards a critical race theory of education. In *Education, globalisation, social change*, ed. H. Lauder, P. Brown, J.-A. Dillabough, and A.H. Halsey, 570–85. Oxford: Oxford University Press.

Mac An Ghail, M. 1988. *Young gifted and black*. Buckingham: Open University Press.

McKinney, C. 2005. A balancing act: Ethical dilemmas of democratic teaching within critical pedagogy. *Education Action Research* 13, no. 3: 375–89.

Nagda, A.B. 2003. Transformative pedagogy for democracy and social justice. *Race Ethnicity and Education* 6, no. 2: 165–91.

Poole, E. 2000. Framing Islam: An analysis of newspaper coverage of Islam in the British press. In *Islam and the West in the mass media: Fragmented images in a globalizing world*, ed. K. Hafez, 157–79. Cresskill, NJ: Hampton Press.

Poole, E. 2002. *Reporting Islam: Media representations and British Muslims*. London: I.B. Tauris.

Said, E.W. 1981. *Covering Islam: How the media and the experts determine how we see the rest of the world*. Vintage edition. London: Vintage.

Solórzano, D.G., and T.J. Yosso. 2009. Critical race methodology: Counter storytelling as an analytical framework for educational research. In *Foundations of critical race theory in education*, ed. E. Taylor, D. Gillborn, and G. Ladson-Billings, 131–47. New York and London: Routledge.

The Times. 2006. www.thetimes.co.uk, 7th July, front page.

Troyna, B. 1987. *Racial inequality in education*. London: Tavistock.

Troyna, B., and B. Carrington. 1990. *Education, racism and reform*. London: Routledge.

Van Dijk, T.D. 1993. *Elite discourse and racism*. London: Sage.

Van Driel, B., ed. 2004. *Confronting Islamophobia in educational practice*. Stoke on Trent: Trentham Books.

Williams, P.J. 1993. *The alchemy of race and rights*. London: Virago.

Wagner, A.E. 2005. Unsettling the academy: Working through the challenges of anti-racist pedagogy. *Race Ethnicity and Education* 8, no. 3: 261–75.

'You got a pass, so what more do you want?': race, class and gender intersections in the educational experiences of the Black middle class

David Gillborn, Nicola Rollock, Carol Vincent and Stephen J. Ball

The article discusses the findings of an ESRC funded project (RES-062-23-1880) which used in-depth interviews to explore the educational experiences and strategies of 62 Black Caribbean parents; the biggest qualitative study of education and the Black middle class yet conducted in the UK. The article focuses on the parents' interactions with their children's teachers and, in particular, their experience that teachers tend to have systematically lower academic expectations for Black children (alongside a regime of heightened disciplinary scrutiny and criticism) regardless of the students' social class background. The parents' accounts highlight the significance of a cumulative process where a series of low level misdemeanours sometimes build into a pattern of seemingly incessant and unfair criticism that can have an enormously damaging impact on their children. Although our data suggest that these processes can involve children of both sexes and of any age, the parents report a particular concern for Black young men, whom they perceive to be especially at risk. Our findings demonstrate the continued significance of race inequality and illuminate the intersectional relationship between race and social class inequalities in education. This is particularly important at a time when English education policy assumes that social class is the overwhelming driver of achievement and where race inequity has virtually disappeared from the policy agenda. Our findings reveal that despite their material and cultural capital, many middle-class Black Caribbean parents find their high expectations and support for education thwarted by racist stereotyping and exclusion.

Introduction

This article draws on the largest ever qualitative study of education and the Black middle class in the UK to explore parents' interactions with teachers and, in particular, their experience that teachers tend to have systematically lower academic expectations for Black children. Alongside a regime of heightened disciplinary scrutiny and criticism, these lower expectations operate despite the parents' professional success, knowledge of the system and support for high educational aspirations. We draw on in-depth qualitative interviews[1] to explore the complex interaction of race, class and gender in making sense of the parents' experiences as they try to navigate the school system and support their children.[2] The educational experiences and strategies of the Black middle class have significance in their own right but also represent a critical case in relation to the wider politics of race, class and gender in education. We explore this context in the next section.

Why Black middle-class achievement matters to *everyone*: there is more to achievement than social class and parental attitudes

The experiences and achievements of Black students are important topics of study in their own right. However, the contemporary situation in England is such that the experiences of the Black middle class take on a particular significance as a critical case that illuminates the intersectional workings of race, class and gender inequality more broadly. This is because education policy discourse in England (in politics and the media) is currently dominated by a concern with social class inequalities and, in particular, the position of White working class students. This focus operates to remove race inequity from the agenda, places White people at the centre of policy debates, and provides the basis for an analysis that shifts the blame for educational failure onto the very students and communities that experience the injustice.

School low achievers are white and British

(Blair 2007)

White working-class boys are the worst performers in school

(Garner 2007)

Half school 'failures' are white working-class boys, says report

(Meikle 2007)

The headlines (above) are taken from national newspapers on a single day in 2007 and give a flavour of how an image of White racial victimhood in education has been created. The use of the phrase 'working class' is especially important and misleading: it is important because more than half the British population describe themselves this way (BBC News 2007); it is misleading because the statistics at the heart of the newspaper stories actually relate to only 13% of the student population, i.e. those in receipt of free school meals (FSM) (Gillborn 2010a, 12):

The interests of the white working class are habitually pitched against those of minority ethnic groups and immigrants, while larger social and economic structures are left out of the debate altogether...there is a fairly consistent message that the white working class are the losers in the struggle for scarce resources, while minority ethnic groups are the winners – at the *direct expense* of the white working class. (Sveinsson 2009, 5: emphasis in original)

The FSM category is used as a crude proxy for family poverty in a good deal of research, mainly because schools have the data to hand and so it is much easier to gather and analyse than more complex and varied notions of social class. There are numerous problems with using FSM status; most working class students do not qualify for FSM and the official statistics exclude students who *qualify* for FSM but do not take up the offer. Far from indicating 'working class' status, therefore, FSM is not even a wholly reliable indicator of poverty. In addition, FSM status is not independent of significant variation between different ethnic groups. Among the largest ethnic groups, White students are the *least* likely to receive FSM but the achievements of this group are the *lowest* of all FSM groups (see Table 1). Consequently *a focus on White FSM students has the effect of removing wider race inequalities from view*: overall White British students are *more* likely to achieve the benchmark level of success than all but one of the largest ethnic groups counted in English educational statistics (Table 1). Within each of these groups girls are more likely to achieve the benchmark than their male counterparts (DCSF 2009).

There is a further twist to how race and class dis/advantages are reported in the media which, once again, serves to advance White interests. As Table 1 illustrates, for White students the combination of relatively high non-FSM achievement and particularly low FSM attainment means that the '*FSM gap*' is much larger for White British students than for any other group (32.5 percentage points). For Black Caribbean students the gap is 12.5 percentage points, a little above the lowest gap (9.9 for Bangladeshi students). This pattern is not new and its consequences for policy and race inequality are clear: '*privileging class inequality has the effect of privileging White interests*...because educational inequalities associated with social class do not appear to be equally important for all students regardless of ethnic background' (Gillborn 2008, 53: emphasis in original; see also Rollock 2007a). The FSM gap is increasingly highlighted (by academics and commentators alike) as further evidence of the disadvantaged position of White students via-à-vis their minoritized peers. For example, *The Guardian* newspaper highlighted two presentations at the 2010 British Educational Research Association (BERA) annual conference under the headline 'Social class affects white pupils' exam results more than those of ethnic minorities – study' (Shepherd 2010). The coverage included two key themes; first that the achievement association with class is a problem for White pupils (and

Table 1. Academic achievement by ethnic origin and free school meal status, both sexes, England 2009.

Ethnic Group[1]	Students achieving 5+ higher grade passes incl. English & maths [2]			FSM gap[3]	Percentage of ethnic group who are FSM	Number (N)
	N-FSM	FSM	All Pupils			
White British	54.3%	21.8%	51.0%	32.5	10.2%	457,346
Pakistani	47.0%	34.6%	43.1%	12.4	31.1%	15,892
Indian	69.3%	48.3%	67.2%	21.0	10.2%	13,291
Black African	55.0%	35.8%	48.4%	19.2	34.3%	12,833
Black Caribbean	42.1%	29.6%	39.4%	12.5	21.5%	7,944
Mixed (White Bl.Carib.)	46.9%	27.6%	42.4%	19.3	23.0%	6,183
Bangladeshi	53.0%	43.1%	48.4%	9.9	46.2%	5,944

Notes: 1. The official tables give results for more than 20 different ethnic categories; those listed here are the discrete ethnic groups with at least 5,000 students in the cohort.
2. The proportion of students in the ethnic group who achieved the benchmark level of achievement (at least five higher grade GCSE passes including English and mathematics) by students not in receipt of free school meals (N-FSM) and those in receipt of free school meals (FSM).
3. The percentage point difference between the achievement of N-FSM and FSM.

Source: original table using official data from DCSF (2009) *Key Stage 4 Attainment by Pupil Characteristics in England 2008/09* (SFR 34/2009) Table 2.

not for minoritized groups), and second, that high and low achievement are explicable in terms of family cultural resources:

> ...one of the reasons why class determines how white pupils perform at school is that white working-class parents may have lower expectations of their children than working-class parents from other ethnic groups. (. . .) Professor Ramesh Kapadia, who led the study, said this may be linked to 'cultural aspirations and expectations, as well as parental support for education. This appears to have been the case for Indian and Chinese pupils for many years,' he said. (. . .)

> Professor Steve Strand (. . .) said the effects of poverty are 'much less pronounced for most minority ethnic groups.' 'Those from low socio-economic backgrounds seem to be much more resilient to the impact of disadvantage than their white British peers,' he said. However, he added that well-off white children may do particularly well because their parents might be 'a bit more savvy about ensuring that they go to schools with similar pupils.' (Shepherd 2010)

The dominant view of race, class and gender in contemporary English education, therefore, cites quantitative data to argue that White pupils in general, and White working-class boys in particular, are the group at most risk of academic failure. *Deep and persistent patterns of overall race inequality have been erased from the policy agenda; the fact that most minoritized groups are out-performed by their White peers is entirely absent from debate.* Meanwhile, both success and failure are deemed to be a function of family- and/or community-specific dispositions. This is an extremely powerful combination of themes; by placing 'poor White people' at the heart of debate, politicians and commentators *appear* to be concerned with issues of social justice and yet the deficit discourse of low aspirations allows them to lay the blame at the door of the very people they claim to support (see Allen 2009; Gillborn 2010a). The real winners in this constellation of discourses are White elites, whose own high achievement is seen as the natural, rightful reward for hard work.

It is in this context that the present study represents a potentially crucial intervention. Contrary to the dominant preoccupation with White students, and especially those living in economic disadvantage, our focus is on the experiences of the Black middle class. Drawing on the insights of Critical Race Theory (CRT), we reject the automatic focus on White people as the normative centre for analysis and, instead, foreground the experiences and voices of people of colour. In particular, we build on the CRT tenet that scholarship should accord a central place to the experiential knowledge of people of colour as a means of better understanding and combating race inequity in education (Delgado and Stefancic 2001; Gillborn 2008; Ladson-Billings and Tate 1995; Lynn and Parker 2006; Matsuda et al. 1993; Solórzano and Yosso 2002). In this case the focus is particularly important because, as we show in the remainder of this article, our data suggest that racism remains a potent force in education; social class advantage (including material wealth and possession of middle-class cultural and social capital that are valuable in interactions with schools) does not provide an automatic ticket to success; and, in particular, parental expectations cannot be assumed to be the predominant cause of underachievement in a system where the expectations of *White teachers* continue to exert enormous influence.

Researching the educational strategies of the Black middle class

Over a two year period (2009 to 2011) we interviewed 62 Black middle-class parents who self-identified their family origins as Black Caribbean. In a second round of interviews, guided by themes that were emerging from the data, we revisited 15 interviewees to explore key issues in greater detail.[3] Conscious of the very different economic, migratory and social profiles of minoritized groups, we chose to focus on a single ethnic group so that we could do justice to the particular context within which our respondents engaged with the education system. The Black Caribbean community has a long and distinguished history in the UK (Ramdin 1987). Many of the most prominent community-based campaigns for racial justice have been led by people whose families migrated to Britain as part of the Caribbean Diaspora (see James and Harris 1993; John 2006; Sivanandan 1990). Nevertheless, this group continues to experience pronounced educational inequity; among the largest ethnic groups Black Caribbean students are the least likely to attain national achievement benchmarks (Table 1) and the most likely to be permanently excluded (expelled) from school (Equality and Human Rights Commission 2010, 313; Gillborn and Drew 2010).

Potential interviewees were recruited via press advertisements, announcements on relevant web sites, and via word-of-mouth; Black professional organisations were a particularly fruitful source. Interviewees were screened to ensure that they had at least one child between the ages of 8 and 18, so that we could explore their strategies and experiences at key points in the education system. The majority of interviewees were mothers who live and work in London but we also made a point of including some parents outside London, including in the North of England. Conscious of the complex debates surrounding the issue of Black masculinities, and wishing to move beyond the popular stereotype of the absent Black father (Donnor and Brown 2011; Reynolds 2010), we made a particular effort to include male interviewees; who account for 20% of our sample. In terms of social class we focused on people working in professional or managerial occupations, specifically those ranked in the top two categories of the eight which make up the National Statistics Socio-economic Classification (NS-SeC); an occupationally-based classification that has been used for all official statistics and surveys in the UK since 2001 (Office for National Statistics 2010).

We used a semi-structured interview schedule that explored our respondents' experiences as children (some of whom had migrated to the UK with their parents) and as adults negotiating the education system on behalf of their own children. Interviews typically lasted around 90 minutes but some went on considerably longer. Interviewees were given the opportunity to express a preference for an interviewer of the same ethnic background; 14 (23%) explicitly stated that they preferred to be seen by Dr Rollock (the team member of Black Caribbean heritage) and, overall, more than 80% of the interviews were undertaken by Dr Rollock. All interviews were audio recorded, transcribed and then coded across the team as themes emerged and were refined using the constant comparative method.

Our research, therefore, questioned people with well paid jobs who have successfully navigated the system. Nevertheless, it was rare to find anyone who felt that race/racism was *not* an important factor in understanding their own experience of the world in general, and, in particular, their children's chances in education. One of the parents' most common concerns was that teachers tended to have too modest expectations of Black children. This is the focus for the rest of this article; we begin with the parents' recollections of their own experiences as school children.

Experiencing low teacher expectations as a child

> ... I am just determined that they are not going to get what I got at school; which was not very much. (Richard, Director, Voluntary Sector)

A concern that teachers tend to have too low expectations of Black children was common across the majority of our interviewees. In some cases the parents (mostly schooled in Britain between the 1960s and 1980s) had clear memories of their own experiences at the hands of teachers who did not see Black children as academic prospects. Gabriel, for example, recalls the crude racism he experienced as a child at the hands of White peers *and* teachers. He describes the 'big shock' he experienced when, as a 13-year-old, he moved to a selective (grammar)[4] school in the English midlands:

> The racism was *ferocious* from the other students in the school and some of the teachers (...) things like calling me names, like 'gollywog' and 'jungle bunny'; putting the blackboard rubber across my brow, marking my face. All day, all day, comments from them. So it was a miserable place... (Gabriel, Education Consultant)

Racism saturated Gabriel's experience of grammar school and some teacher's made no attempt to hide their view of Black students as intellectually inferior. In one incident he recalls that, after initially being refused membership of the chess club, he went on to beat a rival school's top player only to be rewarded with his teacher's surprised exclamation: 'I didn't think *you people* played chess.'

Our sample is not large enough to draw any definitive conclusions about whether such overt incidents were more likely in academically selective contexts, but several of our interviewees reported especially blatant incidents in selective schools and/or in selective teaching groups within mixed (comprehensive) schools:

> ...you would get things like, 'Oh I didn't think we had any Black girls in the A set.' Because even though it was a girls' grammar school they had always been used to the Black girls not always being in the top sets and things like that. (Brenda, Head of Research, Voluntary Sector)

> So I went to an all girls' school and I suppose my experience there was overtly racist basically, it was *overtly* racist. (...) I was put in the remedial [special education] class at school initially and my mum had to fight to get me out into another stream. Because it was just the assumption that you're Black, that's where you belong. So school, I think my school years were a complete waste of time really (...) I wasn't even put in for exams or anything. It was just assumed that we wouldn't, you know, I wouldn't get the results. (Barbara, Child Health Professional)

Robert (who attended a grammar school in the 1960s) recalls growing conflict between himself and teachers against the backdrop of increasing Black consciousness movements in the wider society:

> ...there was a lot of undermining by people who I think were racist and who clearly had no respect for me as a person; who had no respect for the sort of things that I was positive about...black person, black culture, who my heroes should be and so on. Maybe they couldn't help it because of *their* backgrounds. But I found myself in constant conflict with them. And don't forget that this was a time – 1964 onwards – when, if you like, there was an *awakening* of Black consciousness (...) I would call myself, to annoy them, Robert *X*, things like that. There was just a *clash* with authority. But obviously it wasn't one way traffic because it wasn't just *me* railing against them; in a way I was railing against them because I felt that they were very denigrating towards things that I thought were important in asserting who I was... (Robert, Academic in Higher Education)

Conflict with teachers and teachers' low expectations went hand-in-hand for many of our interviewees. Indeed, Robert states clearly that anything other than low expectations would have been so out of the ordinary as to arouse his suspicion:

> ...the teachers also obviously played a part in guiding certain people in the Oxbridge direction. So even though I was one of the brightest no-one ever suggested that I aspire to that. But you know, towards the end of my time there, I was really so disenchanted that if they suggested something like that,

coming from some of them, I would've thought that they were trying to harm me, you know, it was that bad. (Robert, Academic in Higher Education)

Although most of our interviewees did not report *overt* acts of racism at the hands of their teachers, a clear majority reported feeling that, as children, they had faced systematically lower teacher expectations:

> For me secondary school was a positive experience socially, the problems came with the expectations of the teachers on me, they didn't expect much (...) school was more of a social place rather than an academic, there was no expectation of me as a child from the teachers, it was just, 'you're here, let's just take you through the system.' (Cynthia, Teacher)

Teachers' lower expectations were often difficult to pin down explicitly but became clearer at points of selection, when students were placed in hierarchical teaching groups or denied access to high status subjects and examinations:

> I left school with six grade one CSE's [Certificate of Secondary Education: the lower status exam] because I wasn't allowed to do 'O' Levels [the higher status exam] (...) the way the streaming of the school went, that there was one set of people who were destined for 'O' Levels and another who no matter what happened would be doing CSE's and I was put in a sort of B stream, so we knew I'd be doing CSE's, and despite the fact that I felt that when I came here I was so far ahead of the children in my set (...) I felt that it was a survival battle to actually get grade one just to prove that I was capable. (Vanessa, Community Development Officer).

Despite sometimes difficult, even traumatic experiences in school when they were children, our interviewees have ultimately succeeded in attaining professional careers that place them in the highest social class groupings. They have high expectations for their children and are vigilant for signs of possible problems. In many cases they report that, although times have changed and racism is rarely as crude and obvious as in their childhood, low expectations among teachers remain a critical concern.

Parental experiences and the expectations of teachers

> ...you're not gonna walk into the school and someone's gonna call you 'nigger.' But the absence of that doesn't mean everything else is [fine]. It's the subtlety and I think it is more on an interpersonal level now rather than institutional. But of course the people in the institution, so it can become institutional because there's so many of them in the one place. (Jean, Further Education Lecturer)

British society has changed considerably since the post-war surge in immigration from the British Commonwealth but, as our interviewees point out, it would be a mistake to imagine that the relative absence of *overt* racism signals a sea change in deeper attitudes. Crude and obvious displays of race hatred are now rare; gone are 'the signs in windows: "No Dogs, No Coloureds, No Irish" that were almost iconic in their depiction of London in the 1950s and 1960s' (McKenley 2005, 16). And yet anti-immigrant policy was a central theme in the 2010 General Election and one of the new government's first acts was to announce stricter English language tests for new migrants (BBC News 2010). When it comes to monitoring their children's experiences in school, our interviewees are alert for indications of more subtle racism:

> I think the same emotions that drive the racism and the way it manifests itself, the emotions are there, they are the same. The way it manifests itself is possibly more covert now because increased awareness has led to some people wanting to examine what they do and change; and other people wanting to *hide* what they do. So I think it is more covert, it is more subtle in some ways. (Ella, Senior Health Professional)

Academic selection occurs throughout children's school lives in England, and can have a huge impact on their educational opportunities. However, the key points of selection, and the processes that lie behind them, are increasingly hidden. For example, students in primary school are assessed and ranked by teachers who then place them in different 'interventions' that can lead to academic routes or more 'remedial' action (Bradbury 2011). Later, students are assessed (sometimes using IQ tests) on entry to secondary school and may be placed in hierarchical groups that restrict their curriculum and determine entry to low status examinations when they are 16 (Gillborn and Youdell 2000). All of these processes have been shown to disadvantage Black students but none of them are open to parental scrutiny (Gillborn 2008, 2010b; Tikly et al. 2006). As a result, Black middle-class parents have to see through the veneer of pleasantries that often greet them at parents' evenings (where teachers are keen to run through a brief meeting without incident). Cynthia, who works as a teacher herself, became concerned when she read through her child's work: 'Low expectations; work not being marked; *wrong* being marked *right*; no direction.' She continues:

> we go to parents evening and they would say to every parent, 'Oh your children are wonderful, well behaved, they're so polite.' Yeah, I got that, that's my job, I don't need to hear that from you. It was nice to hear but I want you to tell me *academically* what's going on, where they're at (...) And I just wasn't getting that, as long as they were nice and polite, it was okay. (Cynthia, Teacher)

Cynthia's concerns are echoed by many of our interviewees, who suspect that White teachers are content with Black students so long as they do not cause trouble and look likely to achieve a basic passing grade (which will add to the school's profile in published performance tables); they see little or no evidence of teachers pushing students to attain the highest possible grades. Vanessa speaks for many when she summarizes her son's experiences and the minimal expectations that his teachers had for him:

> We had in the final year [aged 16] the expectations from some of his teachers, you picked up that they said 'Well you got a pass, so what more do you want? Where we weren't expecting you to get a pass.' (...) [Eventually] he got a mixture of A stars [the highest possible grade], As, I think his lowest grade was a B for sociology – which upset him because they lost his coursework, his coursework got *mislaid*. (Vanessa, Community Development Officer)

When prizes are awarded and extra resources are allocated, Black students are typically notable by their absence. This trend is visible to our interviewees, several of whom detail occasions when their children's achievements were overlooked in one way or another. Robert (below) was angered when his daughter's achievements were absent from the celebrations bestowed on her White peers: 'clearly she wasn't their blue-eyed person.' Similarly, Malorie points to the racially exclusive composition of a newly established programme for 'gifted' children:

> ... the school was running a gifted and talented programme (...) they selected the young people who they saw as gifted and talented to be a part of this programme and started to do things with them, extended their experiences and opportunities and as I say, found out about it by default. (...) So they chose these young people and do you know what? All of them were White. (Malorie, Education Manager, Local Authority)

> You look at objective things and you make your objective judgements and you see how prizes are being distributed and so on. (...) I remember in one case I actually wrote to the school to point out that [my daughter] wasn't listed in the school magazine as having got a certain award in music, a certain grade in music exams, and they actually wrote to say that it would be corrected and they would put something in the magazine next year. So that was something that I did in one case, but the fact is I couldn't quite understand how it was that *her* achievements were omitted; clearly she wasn't their blue-eyed person. Whereas someone else's comparable achievement hadn't been omitted. (Robert, Academic HE)

Our interviews suggest, therefore, that middle-class status is no protection from the low expectations that research has highlighted as an almost constant threat to the school experiences and achievements of Black Caribbean students (Crozier 2005; Gillborn 1990, 2008; Gillborn and Youdell 2000; Rhamie 2007). In addition, our data reveal the importance of *cumulative* processes of heightened control and disciplinary punishment, alongside the lower academic expectations. This issue is explored in the following section via detailed consideration of the experiences of one of our interviewees and her eight-year-old son.

'*It's like you're trying to break his spirit*': cumulative processes of criticism and control

Drawing on her research with 22 Black British families,[5] Gill Crozier reached the following conclusion:

> ...according to the parents' accounts the young black people in this study have had a pattern of cumulative negative experiences that have often contributed to their demotivation; in a number of cases their permanent exclusion from school, and in most cases leaving school at 16 with fewer qualifications than their parents had expected. (Crozier 2005, 595)

Similar patterns emerge in our data, suggesting that middle-class status, enhanced cultural and social capital, and even a high profile role as a parent representative in school, are no protection from these processes, which appear to run deep in English schools. Rather than present a succession of further brief quotations on this matter, a more detailed description of a single case will more accurately convey the sense of outrage and despair generated by the cumulative damage suffered at the hands of repeated unfairness. The case concerns Jean (a lecturer in a further education college) and her eight-year-old son Kareem.

Jean reports that her son's personality has drawn attention throughout his schooling. Teachers have commented on his 'charisma and charm' but these have been viewed as a problem and Kareem has been portrayed as a bad influence on his peers:

> ...he's been labelled as being charismatic but in a *negative* way. Yeah, so from reception [the very start of formal schooling aged 4], 'Oh he's got this charisma and charm that he manages to lead the other children astray'. So what is it? This is the sort of label that he's been getting. I mean I would have thought that charisma and charm was something quite *positive*.

Over time Jean feels that a pattern of almost continual criticism developed as an over-reaction to the minor nature of the problems and cast her son as a repeat offender:

> ...this has been going on for a while. Little silly things. I'd come in to school collecting him and now [the teacher is telling me] 'He's done this today' and 'He's done that'. And hand-on-heart, he's never physically hurt someone. He's never been aggressively rude and abusive or offensive to adult or child. It's maybe attention-seeking, silly boyish eight-year-old behaviour that I think you should be able to manage if you're a professional.

A notable flash-point occurred when Kareem was selected to attend a class especially designed for Black children seen as at risk of failing. Although this intervention might sound like a positive development, Jean feels that a lack of proper planning and resources resulted from the simple, and erroneous, assumption that a course for Black boys would not require the same level of skill and professional preparation taken-for-granted in other parts of the curriculum. She explains:

> The danger is sometimes, with some of these initiatives for young Black boys, is the only qualification for [leading] an intervention is that you're a Black male. Erm, [pauses]. *It's not enough.* You know, I've met many a Black male who actually [she addresses an imaginary 'mentor'] *keep away from kids at all costs.* Yeah, so this guy (...) You recognise your target group is maybe children who are having some problems focusing, concentration, so actually you [should] come equipped with some strategies to get them on board. And in this one hour session, apparently Kareem disrupted it so bad that [the adult] couldn't continue. What's Kareem doing? He's rocking on his chair, and he might be going [drums fingers on the desk] and making the other boys laugh. Now I wouldn't mind if he got up and kicked you and punched you...well I *would*, but [I could understand the reaction] if it was something *extreme*, but it was *low level*.

In addition to her frustration at what appeared to be an over-reaction from the staff member concerned, Jean also detected that a no-win situation was developing where her son was *always* deemed to be at fault. On this occasion Kareem was disciplined for distracting his peers, but in previous meetings to discuss his behaviour the issue had been reversed, with the accusation being that Kareem was too easily distracted by others:

> I've had this conversation with this man where, you know, one of Kareem's things is to not be distracted by others. Oh. *So* when *he's* doing the distracting and others are being distracted, surely *they* should be spoken to, not to be distracted by him? Now it sounds like I'm being really picky here but - so he gets in trouble if he's a *distractor* and also if he's *distracted*.

The situation came to a head over an apparently tiny matter which highlights the devastating cumulative nature of the problems that can face Black children and their parents, regardless of social class. Once again, the context might appear superficially to be a positive multicultural situation (a project around the election of the USA's first-ever Black president). As Jean explains, her son was highly motivated and engaged by the topic; he produced exceptional work and, co-operating with peers, he won an exciting reward which was summarily taken from him as an additional punishment for a completely unrelated and minor infraction of playground rules.

> ...the icing on the cake was when he did this activity in a class, in his class, and erm, it was all around the Barack Obama stuff, which I thought was

really positive. They did their own election campaign in groups and his lead-ership skills came to the fore, [he] came out with some stuff for his campaign and his group *won*. So their reward was to run the class for the afternoon the following week. And he was so inspired by this Barack Obama. He'd done some writing on him, cut some pictures out, and made a scrapbook thing at home. He'd done this in class as well and was really really looking forward to it and had ideas of what he was gonna do, and then he was excluded from that.

Yeah he was excluded from that.

His teacher wouldn't allow him to do it because at lunch time when the bell rang, he wasn't lining up. He was put in the office. He was put in the office and then his teacher saw him in there and decided not only was he gonna miss his - he missed his play time [recess]. I would have thought that was the sanction for not lining up. Missed his play time but also he wasn't going to take part in the after lunch campaign. (...)

It's like you're trying to break his spirit to a certain extent. Erm, and he's not a crier, my boy's not a crier, but he was crying now that he didn't want to go to school and this had been going on for weeks now.

Jean is a professional educator and was active in her son's school as chair of the governing body (officially the most high profile role avail-able to a parent). These roles might be expected to generate a certain amount of respect from fellow educators in her son's school but this was not the case:

I'm chair of governors and they've just no respect. If there's no respect for me, it translates into this for your kids. And I'm not missing out – I mean obviously I've really *summarised* it – I'm not, he's not done anything that I've missed out. Like he's kicked someone or sworn, he's not done *anything* like that. And I agree some of the behaviour was really *irritating* at worst, but actually I don't think it warranted that repeated kind of... [her voice trails off]

Jean moved Kareem to a new school where his relationship with teachers has been much improved. Her case captures, in painful detail, the cumula-tive damage wrought by a process that showed her son no understanding, and her no respect. At no time was Kareem accused of any major rule-breaking but the sense of continual – often unfair – criticism drove mother and son to a point where neither could continue with the school. Fortu-nately, Jean's personal networks and understanding of the system (her mid-dle-class cultural capital) helped her to secure an alternative school for her son; but the damage was done and continues to be done to other Black chil-dren in the same situation.

It's different for boys?

> I think as a Black *guy* and not a *small* Black guy, you know, the instant perception is of, in the street, is of someone who might be dangerous, might be a little bit violent, might be a little bit angry. I am not the first person people come up and ask the time. (Richard, Director, Voluntary Sector)

The intersection between racialized and gendered inequalities is complex and prone to oversimplification. In terms of academic achievement, Black Caribbean students of *both* sexes are less likely to succeed in school than their White counterparts. However, the average achievements of Black boys are lower than those of their female counterparts and the gap between Black and White boys is bigger than the gap for Black and White girls.[6] Clearly, both gender and race are significant factors. This complexity tends to be overlooked in much popular discussion about race and achievement. As we have noted (above) the educational landscape in contemporary England is dominated by the erroneous assumptions that White 'working class' children are the lowest attaining group and that race inequality is no longer an important issue. When race inequality *is* mentioned in the media, it is frequently assumed that the 'problem' relates only to Black *boys* and the blame is quickly laid at the door of the children, their families and communities:

> African-Caribbean boys are still at the bottom of the league table (. . .) They have failed their GCSEs because they did not do the homework, did not pay attention and were disrespectful to their teachers. (Sewell 2010, 33)

> Black boys aren't being failed; many are failing themselves. Those who went to school in London have their stories about the unteachable black boys who viewed the whole idea of education as effeminate. (West 2010)

These kinds of perspectives trade on the stereotypical view of the Black male as hyper-masculine, i.e. prone to acts of aggression and unsuited to academic study. Black female sexuality has been similarly fetishized (Gilman 1987; Pajaczkowska and Young 1992) and Black young women and their mothers face a range of negative stereotypes inside schools (Mirza and Joseph 2010; Youdell 2006, 119–24). This complex interplay between race and gender is present in the experiences and concerns of the Black middle-class parents in our study. In particular, a strong theme throughout the interviews is the greater threat of stereotyping and exclusion perceived to operate for Black boys and young men – a gendered stereotype documented in numerous school ethnographies (Connolly 1998; Gillborn 2008; Rollock 2007b; Wright 1986). As Kareem's case (above) highlights, even very young Black boys can find themselves singled out for unwanted negative teacher attention. Similarly, Paulette identifies a clear pattern to teacher/student interactions in her son's primary school where Black boys appear to be cast in an especially negative role:

> There were all these issues about him at primary school, 'yes his work is excellent but he can't sit still, he is out of the room, he is out of his seat' – all that nonsense – 'he is answering back' (...) so I felt given the way that the school was responding to him, the primary school, erm given the way that the primary school responded to Black boys: Black boys were always in trouble, Black boys were always outside the head teacher's office, there was that kind of.... Black boys had a particular *part* at that school. I just felt that he was going to hit secondary and I can see it going pear shaped. (Paulette, Psychologist)

Paulette's words are particularly significant because, despite his teachers' judging his work to be 'excellent,' her son was increasingly experiencing a pattern of cumulative criticism (similar to the one discussed above) and in line with the role into which the school cast Black boys as a group. Several of our parents discuss the difficulties they face in balancing a desire to support their sons against such labelling, whilst also being conscious of the danger of dispiriting them by seeming to suggest that the odds are entirely stacked against them. No matter how carefully they try to strike this balance, however, their sons' perceptions are often painfully clear:

> My son said to me this morning...(...) 'if you are a White kid, you can just be a kid, you can just be a child. But if you're Black, you're a *Black* child.' You know, you can just *be*, it's much easier if you're White but if.... Black comes first. And he's fourteen and he was saying that, as an example, that his friends, his White friends just have a different experience, a completely different experience, a freedom that [my son and his Black friends] don't have, that he feels he doesn't have as a Black child. (Barbara, Child Health Professional)

Barbara's teenage son poignantly captures the ever-present threat of racism and racialized labelling in a world where his White peers 'can just be a child. But if you're Black, you're a *Black* child.'

Our interviewees, therefore, are especially concerned that Black boys and young men face a persistent and significant threat of racist stereotyping (against which their middle-class status is little shield). It would be a mistake, however, to fall into the trap of forgetting that stereotyping (although most pronounced for boys) is by no means absent from the lives of Black students of all ages and both genders. As Femi's six-year-old daughter discovered, stereotypes of Black threat and physicality appear to know almost no limits:

> My six-year-old daughter who is yay high [indicates height of a small child] had '*threatened and intimidated*' the teaching assistant. Now, first of all, my daughter doesn't do that at home, so I'm wary; and second, I'm thinking

you're a teaching assistant, how can you be intimidated by a six-year-old girl who hasn't spat on you, hasn't kicked you, hasn't thumped you – what exactly did she do that is so threatening because I struggle to understand a situation where you would be threatened? (Femi, Lecturer FE)

Conclusion

At a time when English education policy is dominated by a focus on White working class students it may seem surprising that research should focus on the experiences of Black middle-class parents. We believe, however, that our interviewees' experiences are of vital importance in their own right *and* as the basis for informing a more critical perspective on contemporary education more broadly. For example, the relatively large gap within the White group, between economically advantaged and disadvantaged peers, is currently discussed (by media and academics alike) as indicating a problem for poor Whites whereas people of colour are assumed to be more resilient or less susceptible to class inequality. But the flip side of the same coin is that the narrow class gap among Black students significantly reflects the lower average achievements of middle-class students in this group. Far from reflecting a relative advantage for Black students, therefore, the smaller class gap within this group indicates the difficulty that middle-class Black parents have in drawing advantage from the greater material and cultural capital at their disposal. This is not because of a lack of commitment, low aspirations or being insufficiently 'savvy' about the education system (Shepherd 2010). Our data show that middle-class Black parents are ambitious for their children and take a keen interest in their education, unfortunately, many encounter an education system that views their children as more likely to cause trouble than to excel academically. Teachers' lack of academic expectations, in tandem with a heightened degree of surveillance and criticism, create powerful barriers.

Notes

1. We employ usual interview transcript notation, e.g.
   (...) = speech has been edited out
   ... = pause
   Emphasized text = original emphasis
   [square brackets] = editorial information/clarification
2. To protect anonymity all names have been replaced with pseudonyms.
2. To protect anonymity all names have been replaced with pseudonyms.
3. The research was funded by the Economic and Social Research Council (grant number RES-062-23-1880).
4. Grammar schools restrict entry to students who have passed some form of academic selection.
5. Crozier's interviewees covered a wide range of social class backgrounds 'from professional to unskilled and unemployed' (2005, 587)
6. In 2009, 54.4% of White British girls achieved five higher grade passes including English and maths, compared with 45.7% of Black Caribbean girls (a gap

of 8.7 percentage points); 47.8% of White British boys achieved this level, compared with 32.9% of Black Caribbean boys (a gap of 14.9 percentage points): Source: DCSF 2009: Table 2.

References

Allen, R.L. 2009. What about poor white people? In *Handbook of social justice in education*, ed. W. Ayers, T. Quinn, and D. Stovall, 209–30. New York: Routledge.

BBC News. 2007. What is working class? http://news.bbc.co.uk/1/hi/magazine/6295743.stm.

BBC News. 2010. English rules tightened for immigrant partners. http://www.bbc.co.uk/news/10270797.

Blair, A. 2007. School low achievers are white and British. *The Times*, June 22. http://www.timesonline.co.uk/tol/news/uk/education/article1969156.ece.

Bradbury, A. 2011. Learner identities, assessment and equality in early years education. Unpublished PhD thesis, University of London, Institute of Education.

Connolly, P. 1998. *Racism, gender identities and young children: Social relations in a multi-ethnic, inner-city primary school*. London: Routledge.

Crozier, G. 2005. 'There's a war against our children': Black educational underachievement revisited. *British Journal of Sociology of Education* 26, no. 5: 585–98.

Delgado, R., and J. Stefancic. 2001. *Critical race theory: An introduction* . New York: New York University Press.

Department for Children, Schools and Families (DCSF). 2009. *Key stage 4 attainment by pupil characteristics in England 2008/09* (SFR 34/2009). London: DCSF.

Donnor, J.K., and A.L. Brown. 2011. Editorial: The education of black males in a 'post-racial' world. *Race Ethnicity and Education* 14, no. 1: 1–5.

Equality and Human Rights Commission. 2010. *How fair is Britain? Equality, human rights and good relations in 2010. The first triennial review*. London: Equality and Human Rights Commission.

Garner, R. 2007. White working-class boys are the worst performers in school. *The Independent*, June 22. http://education.independent.co.uk/news/article2692502.ece.

Gillborn, D. 1990. *'Race', ethnicity and education: Teaching and learning in multi-ethnic schools*. London: Unwin Hyman/Routledge.

Gillborn, D. 2008. *Racism and education: Coincidence or conspiracy?* London: Routledge.

Gillborn, D. 2010a. The white working class, racism and respectability: Victims, degenerates and interest-convergence. *British Journal of Educational Studies* 58, no. 1: 2–25.

Gillborn, D. 2010b. The colour of numbers: Surveys, statistics and deficit-thinking about race and class. *Journal of Education Policy* 25, no. 2: 253–76.

Gillborn, D., and D. Drew. 2010. Academy exclusions. *Runnymede Bulletin* 362: 12–3.

Gillborn, D., and D. Youdell. 2000. *Rationing education: Policy, practice, reform and equity*. Buckingham: Open University Press.

Gilman, S.L. 1987. Black bodies, white bodies. Reprinted in *'Race', culture & difference*, ed. J. Donald and A. Rattansi, 171–97. London: Sage.

James, W., and C. Harris, eds. 1993. *Inside Babylon: Caribbean diaspora in Britain*. London: Verso.

John, G. 2006. *Taking a stand: Gus John speaks on education, race, social action & civil unrest 1980–2005*. Manchester: The Gus John Partnership.

Ladson-Billings, G., and W.F. Tate. 1995. Toward a critical race theory of education. *Teachers College Record* 97, no. 1: 47–68.

Lynn, M., and L. Parker. 2006. Critical race studies in education: Examining a decade of research on U.S. schools. *The Urban Review* 38, no. 4: 257–90.

Matsuda, M.J., C.R. Lawrence, R. Delgado, and K. Williams Crenshaw. 1993. *Words that wound: Critical race theory, assaultive speech, and the first amendment*. Boulder, CO: Westview.

McKenley, J. 2005. *Seven black men: An ecological study of education and parenting*. Bristol: Aduma Books.

Meikle, J. 2007. Half school 'failures' are white working-class boys, says report. *The Guardian*, June 22. http://education.guardian.co.uk/raceinschools/story/0,,2108863,00.html.

Mirza, H.S., and C. Joseph, eds. 2010. *Black and postcolonial feminisms in new times: Researching educational inequalities*. London: Routledge.

Office for National Statistics. 2010. SOC2010 Volume 3 NS-SEC (Rebased On SOC2010) User Manual. http://www.ons.gov.uk/about-statistics/classifications/current/soc2010/soc2010-volume-3-ns-sec–rebased-on-soc2010–user-manual/index.html.

Pajaczkowska, C., and L. Young. 1992. Racism, representation, psychoanalysis. In *'Race', culture & difference*, ed. J. Donald and A. Rattansi, 198–219. London: Sage.

Ramdin, R. 1987. *The making of the black working class in Britain*. Aldershot: Wildwood House.

Reynolds, T. 2010. Lone mothers not to blame. *Runnymede Bulletin* 361: 11.

Rhamie, J. 2007. *Eagles who soar: How black learners find the path to success*. Stoke-on-Trent: Trentham.

Rollock, N. 2007a. Black pupils still pay an ethnic penalty – Even if they're rich. *The Guardian*, Comment is Free. http://www.guardian.co.uk/commentisfree/2007/jul/04/comment.education.

Rollock, N. 2007b. *Failure by any other name? Educational policy and the continuing struggle for black academic success*. London: Runnymede Trust.

Sewell, T. 2010. Master class in victimhood. *Prospect* October: 33–4.

Shepherd, J. 2010. Social class affects white pupils' exam results more than those of ethnic minorities – Study. *The Guardian*, September 3. http://www.guardian.co.uk/education/2010/sep/03/social-class-achievement-school.

Sivanandan, A. 1990. *Communities of resistance: Writings on black struggles for socialism*. London: Verso.

Solórzano, D.G., and T.J. Yosso. 2002. Critical race methodology: Counter-storytelling as an analytical framework for education research. *Qualitative Inquiry* 8, no. 1: 23–44.

Sveinsson, K.P., ed. 2009. *Who cares about the white working class?* London: Runnymede Trust.

Tikly, L., J. Haynes, C. Caballero, J. Hill, and D. Gillborn. 2006. *Evaluation of aiming high: African Caribbean achievement project*. Research report RR801. London: Department for Education & Skills.

West, E. 2010. Black pupils and bad behaviour – Only a black academic can state the obvious. *Daily Telegraph*, September 23. http://blogs.telegraph.co.uk/news/edwest/100055001/black-pupils-and-bad-behaviour-only-a-black-academic-can-state-the-obvious/.

Wright, C. 1986. School processes – An ethnographic study. In *Education for some: The educational & vocational experiences of 15–18 year old members of minority ethnic groups*, ed. J. Eggleston, D. Dunn, and M. Anjali, 127–79. Stoke-on-Trent: Trentham.

Youdell, D. 2006. *Impossible bodies, impossible selves: Exclusions and student subjectivities*. Dordrecht: Springer.

Index

Related titles from Routledge

The Education of Black Males in a 'Post-Racial' World

Edited by Anthony L. Brown & Jamel K. Donnor

The Education of Black Males in a 'Post-Racial' World examines the varied structural and discursive contexts of race, masculinities and class that shape the educational and social lives of Black males. The contributing authors take direct aim at the current discourses that construct Black males as disengaged in schooling because of an autonomous Black male culture, and explore how media, social sciences, school curriculum, popular culture and sport can define and constrain the lives of Black males. The chapters also provide alternative methodologies, theories and analyses for making sense of and addressing the complex needs of Black males in schools and in society. By expanding our understanding of how unequal access to productive opportunities and quality resources converge to systemically create disparate experiences and outcomes for African-American males, this volume powerfully illustrates that race *still* matters in 'post-racial' America.

This book was originally published as a special issue of the journal *Race Ethnicity and Education*.

August 2011: 246 x 174: 152pp
Hb: 978-0-415-67302-0
£85 / $145